CONSERVATION MANUAL

CONSERVATION MANUAL

MARSHALL JOHN

GYAN

Published by

Gyan Publishing House
5, Ansari Road
Daryaganj, New Delhi-110002
Phone: 011-47034999, 9811692060
E-mail: books@gyanbooks.com

Distribution Network
gyanbooks.com
India, USA, Canada, UK, Australia, France

ISBN : 978-81-212-3275-3 (PB)

2nd Impression 2020

Printed at: Gyan Press, Delhi.

Conservation Manual
Author: Marshall John

CONSERVATION MANUAL

A handbook for the use of Archæological Officers and others entrusted with the care of ancient monuments

BY

SIR JOHN MARSHALL, KT., C.I.E., Litt. D., F.S.A.,

Director General of Archæology in India

Published under the authority of the Government of India.

CALCUTTA
SUPERINTENDENT GOVERNMENT PRINTING, INDIA
1923

PREFACE.

THE Manual which has hitherto been commonly used for archæological as well as for other Public Works, and in accordance with which all archæological estimates have been framed, is the *Military Works Handbook*, now in its seventh edition. But as this Handbook was designed solely to meet the requirements of Engineers and Builders engaged on new buildings, it necessarily contains much that is irrelevant and much also that is quite unsuitable for archæological works. In compiling the present Manual, I have made it my object to present the materials in as simple and concise a form as possible and so to arrange and index them that the standing orders, instructions or specifications relative to any given point may readily be referred to. To this end the Manual has been divided into two parts. In the first are set forth all essential Government orders regarding the maintenance of monuments and the conduct of conservation work, the duties of Archæological and Public Works officers and their assistants in respect of it, the principles and procedure to be followed by them, and such other explanations as have seemed to me requisite. The second part contains detailed instructions and specifications on all questions likely to arise in connexion with the conservation of ancient monuments in India. These instructions and specifications are intended to serve as a guide, wherever conditions permit, but to be modified according to circumstances, if for local or other reasons modification is thought desirable.

In the drafting of the Manual I have drawn to some extent on my Pamphlet entitled *Conservation of Ancient Monuments*, which was first published by me in 1907, and I have taken full advantage also of the valuable instructions, particularly as to such matters as grouting, pointing and underpinning, which were issued by His Majesty's Office of Works in the *Report of the Inspector of Ancient Monuments for the year ending March, 1913*. My draft of the Manual has been examined in detail by a joint committee of Public Works and Archæological officers, and many useful recommendations made by them have since been embodied in it. To Khan Bahadur Hira Khan, Executive Engineer, Agra, who was a member of this Committee, my thanks especially are due for the drawings furnished by him for Plates III, VIII, IX, X and XII. To the *Society for the Protection of Ancient Monuments* also, and to Mr. Charles Peers, Inspector of Ancient Monuments in the United Kingdom, I am much indebted for the friendly interest they have taken in the work and for the care with which they have examined the proofs as well as for numerous useful suggestions with which they have favoured me.

SIMLA,
July 1st, 1922.

JOHN MARSHALL,
Director General of Archæology.

CONSERVATION MANUAL.

PART I.

GENERAL.

1. The words 'Ancient Monuments' in this handbook should be interpreted as monuments within the meaning of section 2(1) of the Ancient Monuments Preservation Act (VII of 1904), which reads :— DEFINITION OF ANCIENT MONUMENTS.

"Ancient monument" means any structure, erection or monument, or any tumulus or place of interment, or any cave, rock-sculpture, inscription or monolith, which is of historical, archæological or artistic interest, or any remains thereof, and includes—

(a) the site of an ancient monument;
(b) such portion of land adjoining the site of an ancient monument as may be required for fencing or covering in or otherwise preserving such monument; and
(c) the means of access to and convenient inspection of an ancient monument.

2. The following classification of ancient monuments, both protected and unprotected, has been laid down by the Government of India,[1] and they are so classified CLASSIFICATION OF ANCIENT MONUMENTS.

[1] Government of India (Education Department) Resolution No. 48 of 21st February 1919.

B

in the various *Lists of Antiquarian Remains* issued by the Archæological Department, as well as in the Departmental Progress Reports.

I.—Those monuments which from their present condition or historical or archæological value ought to be maintained in permanent good repair.

II.—Those monuments which it is now only possible or desirable to save from further decay by such measures as the eradication of vegetation, the exclusion of water from the walls, and the like.

III.—Those monuments which, from their advanced stage of decay or comparative unimportance, it is impossible or unnecessary to preserve.

SUBDIVISION OF CLASSIFICATION.

3. The monuments in classes I and II are further subdivided thus :—

I (*a*) and II (*a*) . .	Monuments owned and maintained by Government.
I (*b*) and II (*b*) . .	Monuments owned and maintained by private persons.
I (*c*) and II (*c*) . .	Monuments owned by private persons but maintained by the owners and Government jointly or by the Government exclusively.

INITIAL REPAIRS TO MONUMENTS OF CLASS II.

4. As regards Class II it will often be found necessary to carry out initial repairs, over and above those specified, in order to put a building in such a state that those minor measures will afterwards suffice to keep it in a tolerably fair condition.

N.B.—Because a building is put into Class III, on account of its very dilapidated condition, it does not follow that any measures should be permitted which will tend to hasten its decay. It may still be a monument of interest as long as its fabric keeps together.

MONUMENTS IN THE CUSTODY OF THE ARCHÆOLOGICAL DEPARTMENT.

5. Only those ancient monuments which for the time being are declared to be protected monuments under Section 3(1) of the Ancient Monuments Preservation Act are in the custody of the Archæological Department. But it is the duty of Archæological Officers to bring to the notice of Government any ancient monuments, whether belonging to Government or to private owners, which in their opinion are worthy of being protected by notification under the Ancient Monuments Preservation Act and preserved by Government.

PROTECTION OF ANCIENT MONUMENTS.

6. If an officer of Government considers that a monument ought to be protected, he should address the Superintendent of Archæology who will in turn address the Local Government on the subject.

OFFENCES UNDER THE ANCIENT MONUMENTS PRESERVATION ACT.

7. Cases of offences under the Ancient Monuments Preservation Act should be reported to the District Magistrate for necessary action.

LIST OF PROTECTED MONUMENTS TO BE MAINTAINED BY THE ARCHÆOLOGICAL SUPERINTENDENTS.

8. A list of protected monuments will be maintained by each Archæological Superintendent, in which particulars will be given of maintenance charges and the agency by which the monuments are maintained. Extracts from these lists will be supplied by the Archæological Superintendent to all authorities responsible for the repair of the monuments to which the extracts relate, and correction or *nil* slips will also be supplied each year in order that the extracts may be kept up to date. In the annual correction slips any changes made in the annual grants should be shown.

COST OF MAINTENANCE OF PROTECTED MONUMENTS.

9. The cost of maintaining Protected Monuments is charged to Imperial Revenues, but the execution of repairs and other measures connected with the upkeep of Protected Monuments and of the grounds attached to them are usually carried out through the agency of the Local Administrations.

DUTIES OF ARCHÆOLOGICAL AND PUBLIC WORKS OFFICERS IN REGARD TO ANCIENT MONUMENTS.

R. and A. Department Resolution No. 26-28-2 of July 7th, 1903.

10. The duties of Archæological Officers in regard to the conservation of ancient monuments are laid down as follows :—

(*a*) To advise on the proposals for conservation or restoration works submitted by the officers of the Public Works Department (or other Departments) and to recommend the order of precedence in which these as well as any works suggested by themselves should be undertaken.

(*b*) To submit proposals for the protection, conservation or repair of ancient buildings of interest requiring preservation, which have come to their own notice during their tours.

(*c*) To pass plans and estimates for all works of conservation and repair whether suggested by themselves or by the Public Works or other Departments. It will not be the duty of the Archæological officer to criticise rates, but to approve and advise on the character of the works to be carried out.

(*d*) To assist in the supervision of the works of conservation while they are in progress. The degree of assistance required must depend upon the nature and importance of the work. It will be the duty of the Archæological officer to assist the Engineer with his advice and to bring to the notice of the proper authority any alterations or repairs which in his opinion are likely to affect the architectural or historical interest of the building.

GENERAL INSPECTION OF ANCIENT MONUMENTS.

11. The duty of making regular and systematic inspections of monuments rests primarily with the Public Works Department, who are required to arrange for an annual, or even more frequent inspection to be

made by Executive Engineers of the ancient monuments in their circles. It is the duty of Executive and Superintending Engineers to keep Government fully informed as to the condition of those monuments, whether public or private property, and to prepare estimates for their repair.*

REPAIRS OTHER THAN MAINTENANCE OR ANNUAL REPAIRS.

12. With the exception of the usual maintenance or annual repairs (see para. 36) no work should be undertaken on a protected monument without previous reference to the Archæological Officer concerned.

PROPOSALS INITIATED BY PUBLIC WORKS OFFICERS.

Education Department letter No. 201 211 of the 17th Ma 1913.

13. Before signifying their approval of proposals for conservation or repair works made by officers of the Public Works Department, Provincial Archæological officers are required to consult the Director General of Archæology and to furnish him with a memorandum of such proposals, plans and estimates being also forwarded in important cases.

PROPOSALS INITIATED BY PROVINCIAL ARCHÆOLOGICAL OFFICERS.

Education Department letter No. 323 of August 24th, 1911.

14. Proposals initiated by Provincial Archæological Officers and relating to ancient monuments in British territory or in Indian States under Local Governments are not to form the subject of ordinary correspondence, but are to be printed and submitted in proof in the first instance to the Director General, who, subject to the condition stated in para. 16 below, is to return the notes to the Provincial Officers, who will then submit them to the Local Government concerned.

15. The copy of notes submitted in proof to the Director General should, wherever possible, be accompanied by photographs of the monuments concerned,

*P. W D. Code, Vol. I, para. 314.

as well as by the plans and drawings referred to in para. 22.

EXCEPTIONS TO ABOVE IN CASES OF MINOR IMPORTANCE OR OF EXCEPTIONAL URGENCY.

16. The instructions laid down in the foregoing paras do not apply to proposals for works which are of a minor and unimportant nature, and which do not involve any restoration of the monument concerned or any innovation or addition thereto. Nor do they apply to cases of exceptional urgency, where Provincial Archæological Officers may not have time to submit their proposals or those of the Public Works Officers to the Director General. In such cases they are to communicate to him copies of the proposals made as soon as possible.

MONUMENTS IN INDIAN STATES UNDER THE POLITICAL CONTROL OF THE GOVERNMENT OF INDIA.

Education Department letter No. 323, dated 24th August 1911.

17. The Director General of Archæology will submit to the Department of Education all conservation notes recorded by himself or by Provincial Officers, which relate to monuments situated in those Indian States that are under the political control of the Government of India. The Department of Education will, in its turn, forward them to the Foreign Department for favour of transmission to the Political Officers concerned.

18. Conservation notes drawn up by the Director General of Archæology on monuments in British territory or on those in Indian States under Local Governments will ordinarily be submitted by him direct to the Local Governments concerned.

19. In any exceptional cases the Director General will submit copies of his own notes as well as those of Provincial Officers to the Government of India in the Department of Education for approval.

20. Copies of all notes drawn up by the Director General of Archæology and of those by Provincial Officers will be submitted by the Director General to the Government of India for information. *Education Department letter No. 323 of the 24th August 1911.*

21. In addition to the measures to be taken for the actual preservation and repair of the fabric of a monument the following are among the most important points to be noted on by Archæological Officers when compiling the conservation notes referred to above, or when scrutinising proposals made by Public Works Officers :— COMPILATION OF CONSERVATION NOTES BY ARCHÆOLOGICAL OFFICERS.

(*a*) Reasons for protecting and conserving a monument which is not already on the books of the Archæological Department. In explanation of the reasons, it will usually be necessary to give a brief account of the history and chief features of the monument.

(*b*) Ownership and present use of the monument.

(*c*) Measures to be taken by the Local Government or local civil authorities for protecting a monument under section 3(1) of the Ancient Monuments Preservation Act, including the fixing up of notifications, or for acquiring rights in or guardianship of a monument under section 4(1) of the same Act, or for entering into an agreement with the owner for its preservation under section 5(1), or any other measures which may appear necessary under the Ancient Monuments Preservation Act. Archæological Officers must be careful not to put forward any proposals which are not strictly in accord with the provisions of the Ancient Monuments Act, or which might offend the religious susceptibilities of the individuals or communities to whom an ancient monument belongs. (See paras. 27 and 29.)

(*d*) Ownership and acquisition of land adjoining the site of an ancient monument, which may be needed for its preservation.

(*e*) Delimitation, clearance, drainage, fencing and lay-out of the site.

(*f*) Erection of notices warning the public against damaging a monument. (See paras. 194—196.)

(*g*) Approach roads and means of access.

(*h*) Appointment of caretakers.

(*i*) Inquiries for ancient or local materials for the repair of a monument. (See para. 56.)

(*j*) Reference to previous notes on the same monuments.

SPECIAL WORKS.

22. The conservation notes of Archæological Officers should be accompanied by representative photographs showing the condition of the monument from all points of view before its repair is taken in hand, and they should include full particulars (illustrated as a rule by sketches or scale drawings) of all works such as windows, doors, railings, roofs, seats, or lamps, which are to be restored or newly inserted. No work is to be put in hand without such particulars.

PRESERVATION THE FIRST ESSENTIAL.

23. It may be laid down, as a first principle that, as funds will necessarily be limited, they should be economised in such a way as to preserve, as far as is practicable, as many of the most important ancient works as possible; and, to this end, preservation should be primarily aimed at, and repair attempted only in cases where its advisability is undoubted, and where special funds can be provided for the purpose. Of the buildings deserving repair only a very limited number can be taken in hand in the course of any one year, and many will have to wait, it may be five, or ten, years before they can be repaired thoroughly; but each year the annual work of protecting and preserving them all must go on with unbroken regularity, so that, when the time comes for repairing them, it may not be found that neglect, in the meantime,

has necessitated a greater outlay than would otherwise have been incurred. To this end it may be necessary to undertake certain urgent repairs in order to protect the monument from further decay, and at the same time to arrange for the preparation of estimates for more thorough repairs. Once a monument has been so treated a grant for its annual repair should be provided, in order that it may not deteriorate again before the more thorough repairs can be carried out.

SELECTION OF MONUMENTS.

24. As regards the selection of monuments for conservation, it is difficult, if not impossible, to lay down any comprehensive principles which can be applied to each and every case. First, there are the individual merits of the monument to be weighed; its historic importance; its architectural value; or any features which it may possess of peculiar interest for the social, religious or artistic history of the country. Then, its comparative merits in relation to other monuments in its immediate vicinity must be taken into account; for, in some localities, where there is a dearth of first class monuments, it may be well worth conserving a second rate building, which elsewhere would be allowed to fall to ruin. A variety of particular considerations of this kind defy the application of principles broad enough to embrace them all.

PRINCIPLES OF CONSERVATION.

25. Archæological, Public Works, or other officers charged with the execution of conservation work should never forget that the reparation of any remnant of ancient architecture, however humble, is a work to be entered upon with totally different feelings from a new work or from the repairs of a modern building. Although there are many ancient buildings whose

state of disrepair suggests at first sight a renewal, it should never be forgotten that their *historical value is gone when their authenticity is destroyed*, and that our first duty is not to renew them but to preserve them. When, therefore, repairs are carried out, no effort should be spared to save as many parts of the original as possible, since it is to the authenticity of the old parts that practically all the interest attaching to the new will owe itself. Broken or half decayed original work is of infinitely more value than the smartest and most perfect new work.

LIVING MONUMENTS. 26. In the case of "living" monuments (by which is meant those monuments which are still in use for the purpose for which they were originally designed) it is sometimes necessary to restore them to a greater extent than would be desirable on purely archæological grounds. In every such case the Archæological Officer responsible for the restoration should state clearly in his conservation note on the monument as well as in his Annual Report the reasons which have compelled him to depart from the principles usually followed by the Archæological Department.

RELIGIOUS MONUMENTS. 27. It is the policy of Government to abstain as far as possible from any interference with the management or repair of religious buildings. But if such buildings are of exceptional archæological interest, and if the endowments attached to them are insufficient for their upkeep, the offer of expert advice and guidance or even of financial assistance may be made by Government to the owners or trustees, on condition that the repairs are carried out on lines approved by the Archæological Department. As a general rule, however, the

Archæological Department will not make itself responsible for the upkeep of monuments (other than those already on its books) which are used for religious observances, nor should such monuments be declared protected under the Ancient Monuments Act, except by the express desire of the owners or trustees.

TERMINATION OF AGREEMENTS.

28. It should be borne in mind by Archæological Officers that, even if the owners or trustees of a religious monument are willing to enter into an agreement under section 5(1) of the Ancient Monuments Preservation Act, it is open to them to terminate the agreement at their own discretion after due notice has been given. It is possible, therefore, that Government may be put to much expense over the repair of a religious monument, only to find afterwards that it is deprived of all control over it by the owner terminating the agreement. For this reason it is desirable that in every agreement relating to a religious monument a clause should be inserted providing that, if the owner terminates the agreement, he shall refund to Government any moneys which the latter may have spent upon the monument.

PROHIBITION OF BURIALS, ETC.

29. With regard to such matters as the prohibition of burials within the precincts of protected monuments, the removal of red lead (*sandur*) or *ghi*, or of modern and undesirable accessories (such as lamps, pictures, coloured rags and the like), every care must be exercised by Archæological Officers not to make recommendations which would be likely to offend the religious susceptibilities of people who have an acknowledged interest in the building.

Estimates. 30. Estimates for works to be carried out by the Public Works Department will be submitted by the Executive Engineer to the Archæological Superintendent for his approval and countersignature. Care should be taken that nothing is subsequently added to or omitted from an estimate without consulting the Archæological Superintendent.

Previous notice to be given to Archæological Superintendents before work is begun. 31. When an estimate has received technical sanction and funds have been allotted, the District Engineer will arrange in consultation with the Archæological Superintendent the date when the work is to be put in hand.

Points to be specified in framing estimates. 32. In the framing of estimates care should be taken to avoid ambiguity as to the purpose for which the materials specified in the estimate are to be used, *e.g.*, if so many feet of plaster are shown in an estimate, it should be specified for what purpose the plaster is to be used, *i.e.*, whether for walls, tops of walls, or the like. Should there be any risk of uncertainty, the item in the estimates should be numbered to correspond with a similar number to be indicated on a sketch plan attached to the estimate.

Conservation note to be attached to the estimate. 33. When an estimate is based on a conservation note supplied by an Archæological Officer, the conservation note in question should invariably be attached to the estimate.

Certain repair estimates not permissible. 34. Estimates for Archæological works must not be framed on a plinth area basis; nor must estimates be prepared for quadrennial or quinquennial repairs. Annual repairs are indispensable in the case of all archæological monuments.

35. Henceforth estimates will be framed not only in accordance with the instructions laid down in the Military Works Handbook but with those laid down in this Manual also. Where there is a discrepancy between the two, the instructions given in this Manual will be followed. BASES FOR FRAMING ESTIMATES.

36. Annual repair estimates which include any of the following items :—namely, whitewashing or colour-washing, plastering, painting, underpinning, or restoration work of any kind whatsoever, are to be submitted, for approval and countersignature to the Archæological Superintendent. ANNUAL REPAIR ESTIMATES REQUIRING COUNTERSIGNATURE.

37. Annual Repair Estimates which are intended to be of a permanent nature and to be repeated year after year must also be submitted for approval and countersignature to the Archæological Superintendent at the time when they are first framed and must not subsequently be altered without his approval. STANDING ESTIMATES FOR ANNUAL REPAIRS.

38. In cases where the preparation of detailed estimates is likely to involve much labour, such estimates should not be prepared until there is a reasonable prospect of funds being allotted. In the first instance approximate or rough estimates will suffice. POSTPONEMENT OF DETAILED ESTIMATES.

39. When an ancient monument has once been taken over by the Archæological Department and its repairs started, steps should be taken by the Archæological Superintendent to obtain an annual grant for its maintenance. GRANT FOR MAINTENANCE.

40. The Archæological Superintendent will arrange personally to inspect all works as often as is practicable, and where the work is of sufficient importance to require continuous archæological supervision, he will depute SUPERVISION BY ARCHÆOLOGICAL SUPERINTENDENT AND HIS CONSERVATION ASSISTANT.

SUPERVISION BY ARCHÆOLOGICAL SUPERINTENDENT AND HIS CONSERVATION ASSISTANT—*contd.*

a Conservation Assistant to watch the operations and to help the Public Works Subordinates with expert knowledge and practical assistance. It is important that an Archæological Officer should be present whenever excavations are being carried out in or around an ancient monument.

Education Department letter No. 200 A. & E. of 21st June 1921.

41. All monuments under special repair must be inspected at least once a year, while the repairs are in progress, by the Archæological Superintendent or Assistant Superintendent in charge of them. If for any reason it is impossible for Archæological Officers to fulfil this duty, the facts must be fully explained to Government.

WORKS CARRIED OUT AND SUPERVISED EXCLUSIVELY BY THE ARCHÆOLOGICAL DEPARTMENT.

42. Some works of conservation are carried out exclusively by the Archæological Department. In such cases the Archæological Superintendent will be responsible for contracts and payments and for the adequate supervision of the work. Tools or plant may be borrowed from other agency Departments, but the Archæological Superintendent will be exclusively responsible for the execution of the work.

NEED FOR SUPERVISION.

43. The task of conserving ancient monuments is in all countries a peculiarly difficult one. In India the difficulties which inherently beset it are still further enhanced by the adverse climatic conditions, by the general lack of skilled labour and by the fact that the overseers who are charged with the execution of the work are rarely equipped by training for this class of work. For these reasons it is of paramount importance that the closest supervision should be exercised by District and Executive Engineers on the one hand and by the Archæological officers on the other. The

need for such supervision cannot be too strongly emphasised; for upon it will depend the success or failure of every undertaking.

PROGRAMME OF CONSERVATION.

44. Archæological officers should be careful so to organise their year's programme that they and their assistants may be able to divide their time to the best advantage between the various special works which they have to supervise. Thus, whenever possible, they will arrange for buildings which are situated close together to be repaired simultaneously, so that they and their assistants may be able to watch over the several works at one and the same time.

TRAINING OF CONSERVATION ASSISTANTS.

45. Archæological Superintendents will be responsible for the training of their Assistants and will satisfy themselves that no Assistant is entrusted with duties which are beyond his capacity.

ARRANGEMENTS FOR SUPERVISION.

46. In no circumstances must an Archæological Superintendent ask for funds to be allotted until he is satisfied that adequate supervision can be given to the work by the Public Works and Archæological Departments. If an Archæological Superintendent considers that his own staff of assistants is inadequate for the work in hand, he should submit proposals to the Director General for increasing their number and in the meantime reduce the programme of works.

CONTEMPLATED ARRANGEMENTS FOR SUPERVISION TO BE INDICATED.

47. It will be the duty of the Director General of Archæology to satisfy himself, before funds are allotted, that the works proposed can be adequately supervised. Archæological Superintendents must, therefore, indicate, at the time when they submit their annual conservation programme, the arrangements which they propose to make for the supervision of the works included in it.

SUBMISSION OF CONSERVATION PROGRAMME.

48. The conservation programme referred to in the preceding para will be submitted by Archæological Superintendents each year at the same time as their budget proposals, in order that they may be considered in detail when funds are being allotted.

FUNDS FOR UNFORESEEN OR URGENT WORKS.

49. Should funds be required for any urgent unforeseen contingencies after the submission of the annual programme, application for them may be made to the Director General of Archæology, who will endeavour to arrange for a special reserve for this purpose.

DUTIES OF CONSERVATION ASSISTANTS.

50. If a work of conservation is being executed by the Public Works Department or other Agency Department, the Conservation Assistant will act as the representative of the Archæological Superintendent, and it will be his duty to watch the work during execution and render every assistance to the Engineer or Subordinate in charge of the work and to explain, if necessary, the meaning of the Conservation Notes or other special or general instructions of the Archæological Department, and if possible to solve on the spot any point of doubt as to the intentions or requirements of the Archæological Superintendent that may arise during the execution of the work.

51. He will keep the Archæological Superintendent fully informed of the progress of the work and of any difficulties that may arise requiring his special instructions.

52. The Conservation Assistant will not interfere with or issue instructions to the contractor or workmen, but he will point out to the Subordinate in charge of the work any changes or improvements in the execution of the work that appear to be necessary. He will

record in writing all remarks or suggestions which he may have to make, and any differences of opinion that may arise between him and the Subordinate in charge will be referred to their superior officers. He will also maintain a diary.

DUTIES OF CONSERVATION ASSISTANTS—*contd.*

53. The Conservation Assistant should endeavour as far as possible to foresee mistakes and take action to prevent them before they occur, and it will be his duty to bring to notice, as soon as he sees it, any appreciable departure from the requirements of the Archæological Department as laid down in the Conservation Note, estimate, or specifications, either in materials or in the manner of execution of the work. Such departure from requirements should, in the first instance, be pointed out to the Subordinate on the work, and, if the defect or mistake is not rectified, it should be reported in writing to the Archæological Superintendent.

54. The Conservation Assistant will not be in any way concerned with supply of materials, rates, measurements of work, or payments.

55. He will take charge of any moveable antiquities which may be discovered during the execution of the work and maintain an accurate register of the same and of their find-spots duly entered on a site plan.

INQUIRIES FOR MATERIALS.

56. Before work upon a building is started (see para. 31), careful inquiries should be instituted regarding the supplies of sand, bricks, stone, lime and cement in the immediate neighbourhood. Samples of all these should be obtained by the Subordinate in charge, with their respective prices, and forwarded to

the Executive Engineer for his approval, or, if the work is being carried out by the Archæological Department, to the Archæological Superintendent. The question of obtaining good sand, as hereafter described, is especially important, and samples should be obtained from all pits, rivers, or seashores from which it can be delivered at a reasonable rate. The Subdivisional Officer is to institute inquiries in the district to ascertain whether any old materials, such as old bricks and stones, etc., can be obtained similar to the materials in the building on which he is working, and is to report at once whether such materials are available. But no materials are to be taken from an ancient structure or site without written instructions from the Archæological Superintendent.

NATURE OF WORK.

57. The Subordinate in charge must understand quite clearly that every endeavour is to be made to keep the original portions of the structure in position. Pulling down any part of original work, or restoration as commonly understood (*viz.*, the insertion of new work into the old), will only be permitted upon the written instructions of the Archæological Officer in charge. (See also paras. 25, 26, 68 and 69.)

DEPOSIT OF SPOIL EARTH.

58. The Archæological Officer present at an excavation (see para. 40) will also decide where the spoil earth is to be deposited, so that it need not be shifted again. The place of deposit will depend upon the direction of any future excavations that may be contemplated.

NEED FOR CARE IN EXCAVATION.

59. All excavation is to be carried out with great care, in order that any old masonry or other remains buried in the earth may not be damaged. Any such remains should, whenever possible, be left lying

untouched as they were found, and, if liable to decay through exposure to the atmosphere, should be covered over with sacking or other material and kept permanently damp or dry as may be required.

60. Care should be taken in all excavation work to note carefully the lines of disturbed and undisturbed ground, as much evidence of considerable interest and importance is thereby gained.

PROTECTION OF EXCAVATIONS.

61. The overseer must make careful provision to prevent any water from rainfall or drainage, collecting in the holes or excavations for underpinning, and all excavations are to be protected from inclement weather.

COINS, ETC.

62. The overseer will make over to the Archæological Officer on the spot all coins, curios, pottery or valuables, that may be found by the workmen. It will be the duty of the latter to maintain accurate registers of the find-spots of all such articles and to label and preserve each one carefully. Provided the finds do not come under the provision of the Treasure Trove Act, rewards will be given by the Archæological Department to the workmen finding the coins, etc., at the rate of one anna for any copper coin considered worthy of acquisition and the bullion value of any gold or silver coin. The Archæological Superintendent will decide the amount of the reward for other articles found.

SHORING, ETC.

63. The overseer should carefully strut up or support any overhanging pieces of masonry, fractured door or window lintels. Decayed arches should be properly centred up, if in an unstable condition. Any walls or towers which are in a dangerous state, and are liable to fall down, must be properly shored up

with raking shores, needles, sole plates, etc., in accordance with designs that should be approved by the District Engineer. These posts and shores should be periodically examined to see that the wedges are tight and that the wood has not shrunk or swollen to any dangerous extent.

CONCRETE BEDS, ETC. 64. A firm foundation must be obtained for the sole pieces of the shores, and concrete beds are to be formed if necessary. Needles are not to be cut into the walls except by the direction of the Archæological Superintendent.

SCAFFOLDING. 65. The overseer must assure himself that the scaffolding to be used is of good sound material, and not defective or liable to sudden fracture.

STRUTTING AND PLANKING. 66. The overseer should see that the sides of trenches, etc., are efficiently strutted and planked, and that they are kept free from water by pumping or draining.

VISITORS. 67. Visitors should not be allowed near those portions of the building where works of preservation are in progress, and in some cases the buildings should be wholly closed to the public. Notices are to be erected at all points of approach, and this rule is to be strictly enforced, except in those cases where written permission has been granted to view the ruins.

HISTORICAL EVIDENCES. 68. Great care should be taken in all cases not to fill up or obscure old beam holes or putlog holes, etc., in the walls. In securing wall tops, gable ends, etc., existing evidence of slopes of roofs, etc., must be left exactly as found, and not touched in any way without the instructions of the Archæological Superintendent.

69. Overseers are to remember that every scrap of evidence existing in the building on which they are working—such as broken corbels, string courses, relieving arches, etc.—is to be preserved and not in any way obscured by the works of preservation, and that all new evidence brought to light should be reported.

Replacement of fallen members.

70. In cases where fallen features of a ruined building may have to be replaced, great help may be afforded towards the necessary reconstruction by a careful survey of the débris before any stone is lifted from the ground. A stone, falling from the walls or roof, will naturally come to the ground on a spot as near as possible vertically below the position it originally occupied; and so its place upon the ground will help to indicate its former position. A rough sketch plan of the site should be made, on which the ground immediately around the base of the building is marked off into separate areas. The individual stones can then be marked according to the area in which they lie (see paras. 189, 221). To gather up these fallen stones and to mix them indiscriminately, would cause hopeless confusion to those unfamiliar with the construction of such buildings. These remarks apply, also, to the excavation of sculptures embedded in the débris accumulated around the bases of temples. Very great care is necessary in such cases not to damage the sculptures or the basement mouldings of the temple in the operation.

Completion of works.

71. Immediately after the completion of repairs to any monument, the building and its surroundings should be cleaned and tidied up and any marks that

may have been affixed to stones should be erased. All mortar wheels, mortar heaps, brickbats, rubbish and the like should also be entirely removed.

COMPLETION CERTIFICATES.

Education Department letter No. 200 A. & E. of June 21st, 1921.

72. Completion certificates will be prepared by the District Engineer and countersigned by the Archæological Superintendent, who will withhold his signature if the work has not been done in strict accordance with the instructions given on the estimate. When a completion certificate has been countersigned by him, the Superintendent must notify the Director General of the fact. If for any reason it is impossible for Archæological Officers to fulfil these duties, the facts must be fully explained to Government.

PART II.

DETAILED INSTRUCTIONS AND SPECIFICATIONS.

73. If existing arches have to be completed or taken down and rebuilt, centering should be fixed, and, if considered desirable, the rebuilding should be set up dry and photographed (before continuing the work) for the approval of the Archæological Superintendent. With reference to the orders contained in the M. W. Handbook (Reprint 1918, page 26, sections 27-31), which require modification in the case of ancient arches, specific instructions should be given on the estimate regarding bonding, thickness of joints, mortar, etc. ARCHES, ETC.

74. If buildings are infested with bats, expanded metal or wire netting screens should, wherever possible, be fixed in windows or other openings, and automatically closing doors should be provided, made either of wood or of expanded metal in iron or wood framing. (See paras. 104, 106, 266.) The doors should be opened at night-fall and sulphur burnt inside the chambers in order to drive out the bats, after which the doors should again be closed. BATS AND BIRDS.

75. If the openings are too numerous to be closed with expanded metal screens, or if there are objections

on æsthetic or other grounds to their insertion, bats and birds may be destroyed or driven away (*a*) by stretching piano wires taut across the interior of the building at intervals of about 6 inches or (*b*) by suspending in the openings *babul* thorn bushes, on which the bats tear their wings. Piano wires, which have the advantage of being practically invisible, have been found specially serviceable in keeping pigeons from the interior of large domes. The use of *babul* thorn bushes should be resorted to only as a temporary measure or in places where they will not detract from the appearance of a building.

BITUMITE CEMENT. 76. Bitumite cement is obtainable from Messrs. Winter Bros., 13, Crooked Lane, Calcutta. It is useful for repairing leaks in arched, pitched or terraced roofs, in masonry tanks or reservoirs or in galvanized iron roofs. In all cases care must be taken that the surface to which it is to be applied is thoroughly dry.

BRICKWORK. 77. No modern bricks whatsoever are to be used on any old building without the express permission of the Archæological Superintendent.

78. In repairing brickwork, bricks of the same size and fabric as the original must be used; they can frequently be obtained without difficulty, and at a minimum cost, from old dismantled buildings in the neighbourhood, but this should only be done under the written authority of the Archæological Superintendent. In the absence of instructions to the contrary, the bricks should be laid in the same bond and the mortar joints should be of the same thickness and toned to the same colour as in the old work. Where desirable, the mortar joints should be recessed

about $\frac{1}{4}''$ or $\frac{1}{2}''$ back from the face, but this should not be done except under instructions from the Archæological Superintendent. Great care should be taken to keep the brickwork and joints clean. (See paras. 202—220.) BRICKWORK—*contd.*

79. Under instructions from the Archæological Superintendent spalled bricks may, if their fabric is sound, be mended by using either of the following glue cements :—

(*a*) 1 glue . . . } Mixed with the least possible
1 black rosin . } quantity of water.
$\frac{1}{4}$ red ochre . . }

(*b*) 4 glue
1 boiled linseed oil by weight.
1 oxide of iron.

80. Especial attention should be paid to the instructions laid down in M. W. H. pp. 24—25, paras. 9, 11 (*ad finem*) 14, 16 and 17. SPECIFICATION OF BRICKWORK.

81. Benches and seats of the usual modern type with cast iron legs are an anachronism at Archæological buildings. Where benches are necessary in the gardens or compounds of an ancient monument, appropriate designs should be prepared by the Archæological Officer (see Plates I and II). BENCHES AND SEATS.

82. An image that has fallen should not be replaced on a pedestal or in a niche, unless it is certain that it was originally set there. Endless confusion may be caused by the indiscriminate re-erection of images in the wrong places (see para. 85). CARVINGS, IMAGES, ETC.

83. The repair of divine or human figures is never to be attempted and that of free floral designs only in very exceptional cases. Empty niches should remain

CARVINGS, IMAGES, ETC.—*contd.*

empty, if their images are lost; and the spaces occupied by images in friezes and string courses should, in repaired portions, be left blank. Broken images should not be mended with new limbs or other parts, but old portions may be pieced together, as far as that is practicable. This work should be done by an experienced Archæological modeller.

84. The reproduction of geometric designs is sometimes admissible, particularly in living monuments of the Muhammadan epoch, but each case must be decided by the Archæological Superintendent on its own merits.

85. Any carved stones or bricks or any pieces of tilework that are found lying in the débris on old sites, should be restored, if possible, to their former positions, provided always that no doubt exists as to what those positions were.

CAVE TEMPLES, MONASTERIES, ETC.

86. The conservation of temples and monasteries excavated from the living rock presents difficulties of a kind different from those which ordinarily confront engineers. The notes furnished by the Archæological Superintendent must, therefore, be as full as possible, and must be accompanied by detail drawings of any reconstruction that may have to be carried out.

87. Where the original monolithic pillars or walls have fallen or are badly decayed and where it is necessary to introduce new pillars or new masonry in order to support the superincumbent mass of rock, the Archæological Officer must furnish measured plans and drawings showing the precise position and details of the new pillars and masonry, and the exact amount of chiselling required in order to fit the new stones

into their appropriate places. He will also specify the dimensions of the blocks to be used in the new work. CAVE TEMPLES, MONASTERIES, ETC.—*contd.*

88. In all such reconstructions care must be taken that the new stonework may match in texture and colour, and may be dressed in the same way as the face of the rock immediately adjoining.

89. The joints of the new masonry are to be as inconspicuous as possible, so as to avoid unnecessary contrast with the jointless face of the original rock. To this end, the beds are to be sunk ⅛″ and the borders around them are to be chisel-dressed and not less than 2″ in width, fine tooled, free from any winding and true and square in every respect. The binding material will be cement mortar (see paras. 94 and 96), which will be laid in the hollow of the beds, leaving the joints clear and close fitting (see Plate VII, fig. 2).

90. Especial care must be taken to ensure that the new masonry is carried flush up to the rock above, and that the joint between is well sealed with grout.

91. If the original rock face is weather-stained, an artificial stain (see para. 238) may be used for the new work, but in no circumstances will a body colour or coloured plaster be permitted.

92. Where the original verandahs of caves have disappeared, and in some other cases also, it may be imperative to provide for drainage by cutting channels in the ancient floor and walls of the caves. The alignment of such channels must be shown on a plan by the Archæological Superintendent. They will be as short and straight and inconspicuous as may be practicable. Their width should not exceed 6″, and they must be

CAVE TEMPLES, MONASTERIES, ETC.—*concld.*

neatly and accurately cut and chisel-dressed. Unless otherwise specified, they should be rectangular in section, their tops being horizontal, not arched, where they pass through walls.

93. In no circumstances must the ancient floor of a cave be cut to falls for purposes of drainage. Nor must any hacking of the floor or walls be permitted in the cutting of drains.

CEMENT.

94. Cement will be slow setting, complying with the British Standard Specification of Portland cement. The overseer should occasionally make a test of the material from bulk, by mixing some cement to the consistency of stiff paste, and well ramming into a glass bottle. When set, the cement should neither have become loose through contraction, nor have cracked the glass through expansion.

95. In the absence of specific instructions to the contrary from the Archæological Superintendent, the use of cement on any conspicuous part of a building, for pointing, plastering or other purposes should be avoided, as, if visible, it will impart an obtrusively modern note to the structure.

CEMENT MORTAR.

96. Unless otherwise specified, cement mortar should be formed of 3 parts sand to 1 of Portland cement, mixed in small quantities as required. When used for tamping, the mortar is to be mixed with only sufficient water to make it cling together when tamped. See M. W. H., p. 17, para. 12.

CONCRETE.

97. Cement Concrete ordinarily is composed of the following ingredients, but the quantities should be varied according to local necessities :—

For foundations.—1 part of Portland cement, 3

parts of sand, and 8 parts of clean stone, brick or gravel broken to pass a 1½ inch ring, mixed thoroughly, first in dry state, and again after the water has been added.

For flooring and terracing.—1 part of Portland cement, 2 parts of sand, and 5 stone brick or gravel, etc., broken to pass a 1-inch ring.

See M. W. H., pp. 17—19, paras. 2, 4, 11.

CLAMPS AND DOWELS.

98. Unless the cost is prohibitive, clamps and dowels should be of copper, gun-metal or slate. If the use of iron dowels is unavoidable, they should be heavily galvanized and laid in cement.

CRACKS AND FRACTURES.

99. All cracks and fractures should be the object of periodical inspection on the part of the overseer who should place plaster or glass "tell-tales" across all such defective parts of the walls. If of plaster, these "tell-tales" should be made of Portland or similar cement formed in small oval pats, the size depending upon the width of the crack but generally from 3 to 6 inches long by 1 inch wide and ⅛ inch to ¼ inch thick. If of glass, the glass should be ordinary crown glass about 1″ wide and 6″ long, secured at either end with a pat of cement leaving the middle clear. The stone or brick, on which these tell-tales, whether of cement or glass, are placed, should be thoroughly cleaned in order that the plaster may adhere. These "tell-tales" are very important as evidence of settlements, etc., and any signs of movement should be immediately reported to the Archæological Superintendent. The making good of wall cracks, fractures, settlements, etc., is to be decided only after consultation with the Archæological Superintendent, and no overseer is called upon to deal with such work without the fullest instructions.

100. Narrow cracks in walls may be filled with lime or cement grout. Wider fissures may be filled with lime or cement concrete. Or, if a grouting machine is available, they may be filled with clean ballast, broken stone or granite (passing 1½″ ring), and the grout afterwards forced in to bind the whole together.

101. Unless there are special reasons to the contrary, the grout or concrete should be recessed from ¼″ to ½″ from the face of the wall, according to the width of the crack and the relative coarseness of the filling material. The filling material will be coloured and finished to match the adjoining surfaces.

102. For filling cracks in roofs, lime grout or lime concrete should be used. In special circumstances and in certain localities waterproofing compounds, such as Matex, Medusa, Pudlo or Bitumite Cement, may be used, under instructions from the Executive Engineer, for finishing off the grout or concrete. Before filling, cracks or fissures whether in roofs or walls, should be well cleaned and watered, and the filling material should be worked deep into the cracks, and not merely plastered on the outside. "Winter Bros." cement can only be applied to a dry surface.

DOORS AND WINDOWS.

103. Unless otherwise stated, doors, windows and frames, will be of best teak or shisham wood, free from knots, etc. Drawings of panelled and cross-batten doors and gates of typical Indian pattern are reproduced on Plates III to VII. Frames will be securely fixed in openings by means of rag bolts run in lead and let into the joints between the brickwork or stonework, as the case may be. At least two bolts should be

provided on each side of the frame for every three feet of height (see Plate VIII).

104. Expanded metal netting in angle iron frames will often be required for windows. The frames should be L-shaped in section, and their dimensions should vary according to the size of the opening, but $1\frac{1}{2} \times 1\frac{1}{2}$ inches will be the most usual size. They will be fixed in a similar manner to that described above for wooden frames. The expanded metal or netting will be attached to the frames before fixing by means of a flat iron rivetted to the frame (see Plates IX and X). **DOORS AND WINDOWS—*contd.***

105. When expanded metal or wire netting in metal frames is inserted, the frames should be painted a neutral tint to harmonize with the adjoining surfaces. In the case of white marble buildings or walls covered with ivory tinted plaster, the frames should be painted ivory white.

106. As a rule, windows will be fixed and will not require to be opened. For such doors as it is desired to keep closed, special automatic self-closing hinges or springs or other sufficient door-closers must be provided.

107. Hinges and bolts should always be of the strongest and best quality. Unless otherwise specified, hinges should be of brass; the bolts may be of iron with brass screws. Hinges should be sunk in the woodwork and screwed on with long screws. Each leaf of a door or window should be provided with upper and lower bolts, which should be securely screwed on to the woodwork in a workmanlike manner.

108. Unless otherwise specified, doors will be secured by strong brass padlocks, the rings or bolts to which the padlock is locked being fixed through to the inside

of the door, not merely screwed or nailed on to the outside.

DRAINAGE. 109. Proper provision is to be made for drainage, especially for taking off flood water after heavy rain. Water must not be allowed to stand about in pools or ditches near an ancient monument. The walls of many monuments are none too secure, and the scouring of earth away from their foundations may cause much damage. Drains should be made as inconspicuous as possible, but where stone or brick drains are necessary, they should be strongly built on concrete foundations and should not be liable to collapse or sinking or be in need of frequent repairs.

110. Before the rains set in, special attention should be paid to the roof drainage as well as to that of open halls and colonnades of buildings without adequate roof covering.

FENCING AND COMPOUND WALLS. 111. When wire fencing is employed, the standards should preferably be of stone or reinforced concrete. Corner posts (6″×6″) and struts should be bedded in concrete, and intermediate posts (4″×4″) should be buried at least 2′ 6″ deep. If iron standards have to be used, they must be securely bedded in lumps of concrete at least 15″ square, the top of which should be 6″ below the surface, so as to admit of grass being grown over it. Proper straining posts must be fixed to the angle standards, and wires must be taut and nuts and bolts securely fixed, so that the wires may not become slack. The wires should be sufficiently close to prevent goats from getting between them.

112. If brick or stone walls are erected or repaired around the compound of an ancient monument, the

same principles will apply to them as apply to the monument itself. Care in particular must be taken that the joints of the brick or stone work are clean, that the mortar is coloured as directed by the Archæological Officer, and that no mortar is smeared over the face of the brickwork or masonry.

113. If sunk walls are employed, they are to be constructed as retaining walls; proper weep-holes are to be provided and precautions must be taken to prevent the walls bulging from excess of pressure behind. Adequate drainage must also be provided, so that water may not stand in the ditch. SUNK OR RETAINING WALLS.

114. The thickness of such retaining walls at any given point must be not less than one-third of the height above that point.

115. In the repair of old concrete flooring (see para. 97 and M. W. H., pp. 17—19, paras. 2, 4, 11) care must be taken that any old material which it may be necessary to pick up is discarded and that entirely new material is used by the Contractor. Attention to this point is especially necessary, as it is a not uncommon practice among contractors to pick up a patch of concrete flooring, mix the materials with a little fresh lime and relay them, charging for the work as if all the materials were new. FLOORS AND PAVEMENTS.

116. In places where there is much wear and tear to concrete flooring, *e.g.*, through doorways and passages, it is sometimes advisable to substitute composition blocks or stone-slabs in place of the concrete, and so save frequent repairs and the cost incidental to them.

117. The restoration of ancient stone paving should, wherever possible, be avoided, and should rarely, if ever, be undertaken, unless the monument to which the paving belongs is in first rate condition. In the interior of buildings old broken and spalled flags may often be successfully used again by bedding them in concrete and grouting the interstices between the fragments. In open spaces, on the other hand (*e.g.*, in large courts around stupas and temples) it is generally preferable to relay the fragments on a light foundation of broken stone or brick in mud and to allow grass to grow between them. If, in such situations, the existing fragments are insufficient to cover the whole area, patches of good soil (not less than 1 foot deep) may be left between them and turf cultivated thereon.

GARDENS. 118. The lay-out and maintenance of ancient gardens are subjects which call for special knowledge and experience, and questions regarding them should ordinarily be referred to the Director General of Archæology.

119. Before submitting proposals for restoring an old garden or for laying out a new one in connexion with an ancient building, the archæological officer should satisfy himself that the soil is suitable for the purpose, or that it can be made suitable by the help of fertilisers; and that an adequate and perennial supply of fresh water can be obtained, either from wells or canals or from other sources.

120. Most trees require not less than six feet of good soil in which to grow; shrubs not less than four feet; flowers not less than two feet; and grass not less than one foot.

121. If pits for trees have to be quarried in rocky ground, the rock around the base of the pit (which as stated in the preceding paragraph is to be at least 6 ft. deep) should be shattered with a sufficiently powerful charge of explosive, so that the roots of the trees may be able to penetrate into the crevices thus formed. GARDENS—*contd.*

122. Trees and plants which are indigenous in the district where the garden is situated or which have become acclimatised there are preferable to exotic ones, and evergreen trees and plants are as a rule preferable to deciduous ones.

123. Thick foliaged trees, such as the Mimusops (*khirni*), and trees such as the *Nim* which for other reasons are deleterious to anything growing beneath them, should not be planted in positions where they will overshadow shrubs, flowers or grass.

124. Trees of the *ficus* family, *e.g.*, the *pipal* and *banyan*, and other trees which easily take root in the crevices of masonry, should not be planted in the gardens of ancient monuments. If such trees are already growing in the immediate vicinity of an ancient monument, they should, if practicable and if there is no objection on religious or other grounds, be cut down and eradicated.

125. If creepers are required for covering ancient walls, etc., or in the immediate proximity of ancient structures, those only should be used which are known to be innocuous to masonry, *e.g.*, Antigonum, Quisqualis, "Morning Glory," Tecoma, etc., etc., etc.

126. Flowers, whether annual or perennial, are more costly to maintain than trees or shrubs, and, unless

GARDENS—*concld.* laid out in bold broad schemes and maintained at a high pitch of excellence, are apt to detract from the dignity and impressiveness of the garden and of the monument to which it belongs. Unless, therefore, there are special reasons for introducing them and unless they can be well and carefully tended, their presence in the gardens of ancient monuments is not ordinarily to be advocated.

127. If pathways of gravel, *bajri*, or the like have to be laid down, their foundations must be such (however narrow the pathways may be), that weeds cannot force up their way from beneath. Unless this initial precaution is taken, weeds are apt to become a never-ending source of trouble.

128. In laying out or restoring ancient Indian gardens it is all important to preserve the essential character of the originals, whether that character expresses itself in the symmetrical handling of the design as a whole, in the careful balance maintained between its component parts, in the schematic arrangement of parterres, causeways, watercourses and the like, or in the formal treatment of other features. But it is not necessary to attempt to reproduce with pedantic accuracy the original appearance of the garden in all its particulars by banishing from it any trees, flowers or fruits, etc., which were not grown by the ancients. Since the days of the Mughals (to which period most of the old Indian gardens belong) horticulture has made immense progress, and now-a-days it would be as absurd to refuse to grow Marechal Niel or other modern roses in a Mughal garden on the ground that such roses were not known to the Mughals,

as it would be to substitute the old fashioned Indian beaten earth in place of a far more beautiful lawn of grass. In these matters concessions are rightly to be made to modern taste and the wishes of the community who frequent the gardens. Archæological officers should therefore endeavour to observe the happy mean between antiquarian accuracy on the one hand and æsthetic beauty on the other.

129. Proposals to pump cement grout into the interior of walls in order to consolidate or strengthen them should be made with caution. It is rarely that a void which cannot be thoroughly cleaned out with water can be satisfactorily filled under pressure, since there are bound to be dusty surfaces with which the grout will not make a solid joint. GROUTING.

130. The use of grout under pressure requires experience and careful supervision. Special instructions adapted to each particular case will be given by the Executive Engineer, but generally the following rules should be observed :—

131. Numerous holes must be left in the pointing for the escape of air and for the liquid grout.

132. The pointing must be fairly hard and set on the outer face before grouting is commenced; a period of three to four weeks is usually necessary for this to take place.

133. But where cement has been used for filling the joints at the back of the lime pointing, then grouting may be begun about ten days afterwards.

134. Where a grouting machine is used, the whole body of the wall to be treated should be thoroughly washed out with water (forced in under a pressure of

GROUTING—*contd.* about 15 lbs. to 20 lbs. per square inch), commencing at the top of the wall and working downwards. Great care should be taken that no air, or waterlock occurs in the work, or that any bulk of water is left in the thickness of the wall. The walls must, however, be thoroughly saturated before grouting is commenced.

135. The mixture in the machine is to consist of not more than three parts of sand to one of cement, or as near this ratio as the nature of the sand will allow to flow in the machine.

136. The sand and cement in the ascertained ratio are to be measured on a boarded platform, and roughly mixed in a dry state. *Three buckets* of water should then be poured into the container, and while the blades are made to revolve rapidly the mixed cement and sand should be gradually shaken in until the grout becomes creamy in consistency. It should not be too fluid, and the overseer should aim at getting a fairly thick grout forced into the cavities under high pressure, rather than a very thin grout under low pressure. The sand used should not be very coarse, but of finer grains than that used for pointing; it must be perfectly clean and free from dusty particles.

137. The grouting of cavities should be commenced at the base of the wall, and no more should be treated at one time than will approximately correspond to the capacity of the container. This can be estimated when the walls are being washed out.

138. The openings left in the pointing should be fitted with ordinary wooden taps with the ends inserted well into the cavities or the prepared holes left in the lime pointing at the junction of bedding and

heading joints, and the space round the circumference of each tap closed up with damp clay. The nozzle of the feed pipe should be inserted at some convenient point above the level at which it is estimated the grout will rise in the wall. GROUTING—*contd.*

139. When the pressure is turned on, the grout, as it fills up the cavity and rises in the wall, will flow out of the orifices of the taps, and these should then be successively turned off, the process being continued until the grout in the container is exhausted. Care must be taken that the grout does not run down the wall or in any way show on the face.

140. Each grouting point should be fed twice from the machine; and each tap, when once charged with cement grout, either from the machine direct or by percolation from other grouting holes, should be well cleared with a wire before the grout has had time to set in it.

141. The pressure obtained on the machine should, as a rule, be not less than 25 lbs. nor more than 35 lbs. per square inch, and if the above precautions are taken, this should have no bad effect upon the lime pointing (but see para. 150). When the work can be made good with a lower pressure, the above pressure need not be maintained. In no case should the pressure exceed 35 lbs. per square inch. The overseer should carefully examine the pointing after the grout is forced in, and, if it shows signs of being disturbed, the pressure on the machine should be reduced.

142. If any of the lime pointing has been once "started" from the stone faces, cracked by the

GROUTING—*contd.* pressure of the cement grout, the joints must be cut out and made thoroughly good and sound with fresh pointing.

143. In hand grouting the proportions of cement to sand will depend both upon the character of the voids to be filled and upon the degree of fineness of the sand. If the voids are large, one part of cement to two parts of sand may be used, but if small, then the proportion of sand should not exceed one part, and sometimes, particularly in ashlar work, neat cement should be used. In any case it is important to keep the cement and sand thoroughly mixed by continually shaking the can in which the grout is held.

144. A convenient method of pouring in grout is to use an ordinary garden water can (without the rose) with a long narrow neck, the orifice being $\frac{3}{8}$ inch or $\frac{1}{2}$ inch in diameter. The best method of getting the liquid into the wall is to use a cow's horn, inserting the smaller orifice in the wall, but if this is not available, either small cups of damp clay formed on the outside of the grouting hole or handmade funnels of tin or zinc can be substituted.

145. It is necessary to leave, above the grouting hole, another small hole for the escape of air while grout is being poured in, and, in order to make the latter flow more freely, it should be agitated by a thin piece of wire inserted right into the cavity of the stone-work.

146. Every effort should be made to utilise a grout with as large an admixture of sand as is possible, so long as it is consistent with good workmanship.

147. Grouting machines are to be in charge of an Archæological Officer and are to be operated by four men (see Plate XI). GROUTING—*contd.*

148. Fix the pan on a firm bed with a slope so that the delivery end is 6 inches below the other. If the grouting is to be done near the top of a high wall the pan should be suspended from a pulley by a rope passing through the four holes provided for the purpose in the rims.

149. Remove the cover of the grouting pan and connect the air compressor to the pan with the length of hose provided.

150. Two of the men should pump air into the compressor until 35 lbs. per square inch is attained, and the pressure should not be allowed to fall below 25 lbs. per square inch for ordinary cases. Where, however, the wall is thin or weak, the pressure should be reduced to 12 lbs. or 15 lbs. per square inch.

151. Two other men should, in the meantime, mix the cement and sand as above described and place it in the pan. While the third man mixes, the fourth should replace the cover, connect the delivery hose to the pan and insert the nozzle into the hole left for grouting, well ramming round it with stiff puddle clay.

152. The valve on the top of the compressor should first be opened, then that on top of the pan, and lastly the delivery tap. The grout will be quickly forced into the wall, but the mixing blades should be rapidly rotated until the contents of the pan are nearly exhausted. When this occurs (being ascertained by the decreased effort required), the valve on the top of the air compressor should be gradually closed in order

GROUTING—*contd.* to avoid the loss of pressure occasioned by the air escaping through the empty pan, for in no case should air be blown into the grouting hole.

153. The fourth man, who operates the nozzle of the delivery pipe, should watch for any stoppage that occurs in the flow of the grout. This is easily ascertained by the fact that the hose vibrates considerably while the grout is discharging, and if the vibration suddenly ceases before the contents of the pan are exhausted, it indicates that either the nozzle is choked or that the cavity is air-locked. In either case the delivery tap should be immediately turned off, as, if the latter condition is the cause of the stoppage, the face of the wall is liable to be blown out, or the nozzle end of the hose will be forced out violently and the grout will discharge on to the wall.

154. Care must be taken that the delivery hose does not sag, as otherwise the grouting is liable to solidify. If it does choke, it can be cleared out with a long $\frac{5}{16}$ inch round rod.

155. In cases where a wall is weak, or a thin skin of facing material is bonded to a main wall, it must be efficiently boarded and strutted into position before the grouting is commenced.

156. The grouting pan should be cleaned out with water if it is not to be used within two hours of a previous discharge, and the contents forced out under pressure. The Archæological Officer is expected to take great care of the machine, keep the parts properly oiled, and prevent the grout from solidifying either externally or internally.

157. Grout is liable to get into the eyes of the man who operates the nozzle, and as it is very painful and dangerous, the Archæological Officer is to provide spectacles with side protectors, and is to insist upon their being worn. A small quantity of olive oil is to be kept on the site and is to be applied to the eyes of any man who is affected by an accidental discharge of grout. GROUTING—*concld.*

158. In the repair of inlay work (*pietra dura*) the greatest care is necessary in order to ensure that the new stones fit exactly, and that the edges of the existing groundwork are not scraped or chipped. The following is the process to be followed. At the outset a tracing on a thin sheet of mica is taken of the patch to be filled, and the tracing is then cut out carefully and its accuracy tested in order to ensure a perfect fit. When the mica pattern is found to be a true fit, it is then reproduced in thin sheet tin by means of a pair of tinman's scissors. The tin plate is next glued with *lac* to the surface of the stone out of which the piece of inlay is to be carved, and the rough inlay block is then mounted for convenience on a wooden pedestal about 1′ 6″ high and held rigidly in a slot at the top by means of a wedge. The pedestal, which is about 4 inches square in section, is fitted into a heavy stone base to keep it steady. INLAY WORK (*PIETRA DURA*).

159. The fret cutting is done by means of a plain soft iron wire (20 B. W. G.) mounted on a split bamboo bow. A weight is attached to the point of the bow to maintain the proper pressure on the stone. Solid patterns are cut by working the bow like a fret-saw, and if the required pattern has a hole

INLAY WORK—*contd.*

in the centre, a hole is likewise bored through the stone and the wire of the bow passed through it before stringing. The inlay blocks are cut on the slant, *i.e.*, with an inward slope of about 15 degrees on the edges to facilitate the fitting. When properly shaped the edges are finished on a '*san*' or emery wheel, which is a composition of emery powder and *lac* in the proportion of 2 to 1. The edges of the pierced work are also finished off with a file made of the same emery composition reinforced with an iron wire core.

160. After removing the tin pattern, the piece of inlay is tested for size and corrected by filing until it is an exact fit. The edges are then roughened so as to grip the cement, and the piece is embedded in the recess with a special cement, the ingredients of which are given below, and driven home by means of a light wooden mallet. The surplus cement having been removed, the inlay is allowed to set for at least a week, after which the surface is cleaned and rubbed with a '*thapi*' made of emery powder and *lac* and washed with water.

161. The ingredients of the cement are :—

White lime of marble	½	seer
Powdered marble	6	chittaks.
Burnt zinc powder	5	,,
Gum	1	,,
'*Gur*'	1	,,
'*Dal urd*'	2	,,
'*Patacha*'	1	,,
'*Mastagi*'	½	,,
'*Tukhm-i-Balanga*'	½	,

162. The gum is first soaked in water and the other ingredients are ground in the gum water to form a thick paste. The above quantity of cement takes two men two days to prepare. When ready, it is kept in earthen pots well soaked in water and taken out as required. The cement will remain fresh for a week or ten days. INLAY WORK—*contd.*

163. The following is a list of the stones commonly used in Indian 'pietra dura':—

Serial No.	English.	Hindustani.	Where procurable.
1	Agate	Sang-i-Gawa. . .	Banda.
2	„	Sang-i-Ghori. . .	Banda and Jubbulpore.
3	„	Sang-i-Pangban . .	Sabalgarh (Gwalior).
4	Black marble . .	Sang-i-Musa . .	Alwar.
5	Bloodstone . .	Sang-i-Dogasra . .	Jubbulpore.
6	„ . . .	Sang-i-Gad . . .	Ditto.
7	„ . . .	Sang-i-Pitonia . .	Jubbulpore and Chalisgaon.
8	Carbuncle, Garnet .	Sang-i-Tambra . .	Jaipur.
9	Carnelian . . .	Sang-i-Aqiq . . .	Cambay.
10	Conchshell . . .	Sankh	Ceylon and Dwarka.
11	Coral	Munga . . .	....
12	Glass	Sang-i-Sitara . .	....
13	Jasper . . .	Sang-i-Badal . .	Jubbulpore.
14	„	Sang-i-Galahra . .	Ditto.
15	„	Sang-i-Jaiswar . .	Ditto.
16	„	Sang-i-Ratak . .	Gwalior.
17	„	Sang-i-Tilai, light yellow or gold (selected out of Ratak).	....

INLAY WORK—*concld.*

Serial No.	English.	Hindustani.	Where procurable.
18	Jasper . . .	Sang-i-Udha . .	Jubbulpore.
19	Lapislazuli . . .	Sang-i-Lajward . .	(Market Delhi).
20	Malachite . . .	Dana-i-Farang . .	Russia (Market Bombay).
21	Marble (white) . .	Sang-i-Marmar . .	Jaipur and Makrana in Jodhpur.
22	Mother-of-pearl . .	Sip	Goa and Ceylon.
23	Onyx	Sang-i-Lahsania . .	Broach.
24	Serpentine . . .	Sang-i-Margaz . .	Mysore.
25	Shell	Kauri	Any bazar.
26	Turquoise . . .	Firoza	Tibet and Persia.
27	....	Sang-i-Abri . . .	Jessalmer.
28	....	Sang-i-Ajuba . .	Sabalgarh (Gwalior).
29	....	Sang-i-Chitla . .	Narbada river.
30	....	Sang-i-Gudaria . .	Gwalior.
31	....	Sang-i-Khattu . .	Jessalmer.
32	....	Sang-i-Simaq . .	Arabia.
33	....	Sang-i-Zahrmuhra or Sang-i-Paizahrmuhra.	Ajmer and China.

IRON BARS, ETC. 164. When iron bars, grills, grates, dowels, etc., are found to be splitting the stones in which they are fixed, they are to be cut off close to the stonework, and the remaining portion carefully drilled out. If the bars, grills, etc., are old and merit preservation, copper, gun metal or rustless steel ends can be welded or rivetted to the old iron. Where old iron-work set in lead is found to be detrimental to old stonework, etc., the lead is to be carefully drilled and cut out, and the iron re-run in with black rock sulphur.

165. For the preservation of bright iron or steel work in interiors the armour preservation liquid supplied by Messrs. Pinchin, Johnson and Company, Limited, Minerva House, 26 and 27, Bevis Marks, E.C., may be brushed on direct. **IRON PRESERVATIVE.**

166. For the preservation of exterior iron and steel work three coats of boiled linseed oil may be applied, each of the last two only after the previous one has thoroughly dried. Messrs. Pinchin, Johnson and Company Limited's, "Syronite," may, on instructions from the Archæological Superintendent, be employed instead. This liquid can only be used in direct contact with the iron; all loose rust and old oil or paint must first be cleaned off. Should rust still remain after cleaning, a first coat of the liquid will make the rust shed. A second coat should then be given. If the Archæological Superintendent is in doubt as to the best method of preserving any particular piece of iron or other metal work, he should consult the Archæological Chemist.

167. If it is desirable to paint new iron work, such as fences or screen frames, the instructions laid down in M. W. H., p. 51, paras. 19—21, will be followed.

168. When modern lime or cement pointing has to be cut out from old joints and stone faces on any building, great care is to be taken that the edges and surfaces of the stones are not touched with the chisel. When the cement pointing is hard and compact, a very small chisel is to be used, and the centre only of the cement joint cut out, after which the sides of the joints where the cement adheres, are to be picked off with a steel tool, but without the use of the hammer. **JOINTS: CUTTING OUT AND CLEANING OF—**

JOINTS: CUTTING OUT AND CLEANING OF—*contd.*

169. Where the joints of ashlar work are very bad, and the old lime mortar found to be quite perished, the clearing of the joints is to be proceeded with as far as the tools and size of the joints allow, but no actual pointing is to be done until the condition of the old work has been reported upon. In this raking out, the stones must not be allowed to fall through want of support, but must be held in position by means of temporary wooden wedges.

170. When the joints of the ashlar work are very fine, and the mortar in them loose or perished, they are to be cleared by the use of a tool, made from thin hoop-iron, cut with a saw edge on one side. With this the joints are to be sawn out as deeply as possible.

LIME.

171. Each consignment of lime should be examined and tested as it arrives, and any defects in quality should be immediately reported. The lime is to be thoroughly screened to get rid of any dangerous or refractory lumps.

LIME MORTAR.

172. For making lime, stone or kankar is burned in kilns as described in M. W. H., para. 3, pages 15 and 16. The former is then slaked and the latter is usually ground dry in a mill passing through a sieve of 64 meshes to the square inch.

173. Stone-lime mortar does not set unless it is mixed with sand, *surkhi* (pounded bricks) or cinders, in a proportion to be fixed according to the quality of the lime. The usual proportion is 1 : 2 measured dry. For quality of sand, *surkhi* and cinders see paras. 6, 7 and 8 of M. W. H., page 16.

174. Kankar being composed in part of clay does not, unless it happens to be unusually pure, require other substances to be mixed with it.

175. For the making of lime nodular (*bichhua*) kankar of fair quality dug from the fields is recommended. Hard road metal and washed kankar collected from ravines are not suitable. Kankar containing from 8 to 30 per cent. of clay is the best, but all kankar must be thoroughly cleansed and broken to $1\frac{1}{2}''$ gauge before laying it in the kiln for burning. LIME MORTAR—*contd.*

176. For making lime mortar, kankar lime is mixed in a trough according to the requirements of the day, as much water being added as will make it into a stiff paste. Stone lime with its ingredients is first mixed dry on a platform and then with water in a trough.

177. As a rule the lime is soaked in water in a trough at evening time and is mixed and used on the day following; but if required for immediate use, it should be passed wet through a mortar mill for at least 2 hours before use.

178. Unused mortar should not be allowed to set in the trough or on the ground. Any mortar that has remained in the trough for more than 24 hours is to be thrown away.

179. After removal from the kiln lime should be stored in large heaps in properly covered sheds. Stone lime should be made into mortar and used as soon as possible after it is slaked, but kankar lime can be stored in sheds for a long time after it is ground dry.

180. The mortars above described are suitable for fine joint masonry or $\frac{1}{2}''$ thick plaster work, but are unsuitable for wide joint brickwork, rubble stone masonry, and thick plaster work. For the latter class of works, which frequently have to be carried out in the conservation of ancient monuments, the

LIME MORTAR—*concld.*

best course is to grind the kankar lime wet after its removal from the kiln without any previous dry grinding. The amount of grinding required will vary according to the nature of the work, *i.e.*, the grinding will be longer for fine class work and shorter for coarse work.

181. Lime mortar of which the tensile strength is less than 100 lbs. per square inch is not to be used in conservation works. A practical and quick way of testing lime mortar on the work itself is to take a handful of mortar from the trough and, after a minute or two, to wash it off the hand; if the skin is left rough after washing, the mortar may be considered fit for use.

LIMEWASH.

182. The use of limewash or paint is strictly forbidden except under written instructions from the Archæological Superintendent. Where the face of stonework has to be covered with limewash the work is to be done as follows:—Badly decayed stone must first be carefully brushed in order to remove loose particles (the chisel must not be used). The face of the stone must then be treated with a coating of limewash applied with a brush. The limewash is to be made to the consistency of cream in the proportion of 8 or 9 of lime to 1 of sand, to give it texture. The wash may be treated with colouring matter, where necessary, to match the various stones, and when the stone work varies in colour, several pails of different tints are to be mixed and applied as required. See M. W. H., pp. 34-35, paras. 2-9.

LIMEWASH, REMOVAL OF—

183. If it is contemplated to remove limewash from an old surface, precaution must be taken to prevent injury to any inscriptions, relief or painting beneath. Limewash may often be removed by

brushing with native soap and water, or light sponging in the case of painted or delicate surfaces, but, if it will not yield to this treatment, a weak solution of nitric acid (not stronger than 1 : 10) or, in caseswhere the action of nitric acid may be deleterious, of acetic acid, may be used, followed by a thorough washing down with water in which a little carbonate of soda has been dissolved. Acid, however, must not be used for the removal of limewash from marble or limestone, the surface of which is disintegrated by it. Kerosine oil is effective in removing limewash off tilework. LIMEWASH, REMOVAL OF—*contd.*

184. The instructions given in M. W. H., p. 34, para. 1, for the scraping of walls, etc., are not to be followed. In certain cases scraping may be resorted to under instructions from the Archæological Superintendent, but it should be done by means of bamboo, not iron, scrapers.

185. Recommendations for the wholesale removal of limewash on buildings which are still in use for religious purposes should be made with caution and with due regard to the fact that many communities have a strong predilection for such limewash.

LINTELS, BROKEN.

186. Broken lintels or beams should be supported by stirruping them from above, or, if that is impracticable, by inserting R. S. joists beneath; but it should always be borne in mind that such metal supports necessarily detract from the appearance of a building and that they ought, if possible, to be avoided. On the other hand, if a broken lintel is carved or otherwise decorated, it is far better to preserve it *in situ*

LINTELS, BROKEN—*contd.*

by means of R. S. joists or other foreign supports than to remove it to a museum and substitute a plain new lintel in its place. For various methods of employing steel supports, see Plates XII and XIII.

187. In laying a rolled steel joist or angle iron, underneath a broken lintel it should first be thoroughly cleaned and then the whole be painted with cement, laid in cement, and grouted. The outer exposed surfaces can subsequently be cleaned of cement, treated with linseed oil, and painted.

188. In cases where a pier, not forming part of the original design, has to be introduced, it should be made quite clear that it is a later addition, without however rendering it obtrusive by pointing or by other purely modern devices. Such piers should be of plain ashlar masonry or such other material as the Archæological Officer may prescribe. They should be square in plan and as slender as the load they have to bear will permit. The masonry should be chisel-dressed and the joints should not exceed ¼″ in thickness. The mortar in the joints should be coloured to match the adjoining surfaces. In certain cases the method of construction laid down in paras. 87-91 (Cave Temples) should be followed.

MARKING OF STONES.

189. When dismantling masonry, previous to rebuilding, it may be necessary to mark or number the old stones, so as the more readily to replace them in their original positions. In doing this care should be taken not to incise the numbers or to apply to the exposed surfaces of the stones any oil paint or other pigment or stain which will be difficult to remove again.

The simplest plan is to number the stones on their faces with chalk and photograph them before dismantling. After dismantling, the stones should be renumbered on the back (or on some other surface which will not show afterwards) in paint or other durable medium. MARKING OF STONES—*contd.*

190. In certain localities and in certain conditions "Matex" may be used for waterproofing roofs or repairing cracks and fissures. Concrete is a good surface on which to apply it. Owing to its black colour, however, it should not be used in any exposed positions, where it is likely to offend the eye. The covering capacity of Matex is about 1 lb. to 2 square feet. It has about the same consistency as putty and is spread over the surface with a putty knife or trowel. "Matex" is obtainable from Messrs. Skippers and Co., Ltd., 86-1, Clive Street, Calcutta. "MATEX."

191. In damp climates (*e.g.*, parts of Kashmir) it is sometimes necessary to waterproof cement and cement mortar. For this purpose "*Medusa*" and "*Pudlo*" *Waterproofing Compounds* may be used. They are to be mixed with dry Portland cement in the following manner:— "MEDUSA" AND "PUDLO" WATERPROOFING COMPOUNDS.

192. Spread out 25 lbs. of the dry cement to an even thickness of 1 inch, and over this sprinkle ½ lb. of the "Medusa" or "Pudlo" composition by means of a fine sieve or a flour dredger (similar to a pepper box), turning the cement over while sprinkling. When all the "Medusa" or "Pudlo" is on the cement, the mixture is to be turned over at least 10 times until it presents a uniform colour and not a grain of white

"MEDUSA" AND "PUDLO" WATERPROOFING COMPOUNDS—*contd.*

powder can be seen. This is then to be passed through a very fine sieve to remove all lumps.

193. For waterproof mortar, 25 lbs. of the cement treated with the "Medusa" or "Pudlo" as specified is to be put with an amount of sand that would be contained in a box, open top and bottom, the inside dimensions of which are 12 inches by 12 inches by 9 inches (the sand to be struck level). Turn the cement and sand several times over, adding only enough water through a rose nozzle to make a fairly stiff mortar, which is to be used at once for rendering. All mixing to be done on a close-boarded platform.

NOTICE BOARDS.

194. Notice Boards warning the public against damaging protected monuments or for other purposes should be conspicuous enough to attract attention but not such as to be an eyesore; nor should they disfigure the monument by being set up on the face of it or directly in front of it. The narrowest part of the approach to the precincts is, in most cases, the best place for their erection.

195. For such notices, the best material is white metal with lettering cast in relief. If enamelled iron, which is less durable, is used, the ground should be in dark blue or black enamel and the lettering in white.

196. If notice boards are to stand in the open, the face of the notice should be protected by a sloping *chajja* or weather board, 4″ to 5″ wide which can conveniently be made by turning down the upper edge of the metal sheeting. A specimen of a suitable and

cheap form of standard notice board is illustrated in Plate XIV. NOTICE BOARDS.—*contd.*

PAINTINGS.

197. The task of cleaning ancient fresco or tempera-paintings or of removing whitewash, etc., from their face is a peculiarly difficult one, and should only be performed under the supervision of an expert. The Archæological Chemist should invariably be consulted by Archæological Officers and his advice taken as to the treatment to be adopted.

PLASTER STUCCO.

198. The restoration of plaster stucco on walls and ceilings is rarely admissible, and is to be carried out only under instructions from the Archæological Superintendent. Broken, damaged or loose plaster may be preserved with the help of lime grout or, in some cases, of plaster of Paris injected into the hollow cavities behind the loose plaster and by applying a neat fillet of lime mortar round the broken edges, care being taken that the cavities and edges are first washed clean with water. The mortar for the fillets is to be made as specified in para. 207 below for "pointing," with the addition of one part of cement to 9 parts of lime. The mortar is to be worked well into cavities, trowelled to an angle of 40° and finished as specified for "pointing" in para. 209, care being taken in all cases that the coarse grit shows clean and sharp on the surface.

199. On terraces, roofs, and domes, old plaster must be maintained in repair in order to keep them watertight. But in such positions the new plaster should be coloured to match, as nearly as possible, the old work.

PLASTER STUCCO —*contd.*

200. A mixture that has been found successful for this purpose, and which can be varied to match most discolourations, is as follows:—

Kankar lime	25	Seers
Cement	$2\frac{1}{2}$	"
Black slag from brick kilns roughly ground	$7\frac{1}{2}$	"
Black colouring matter extracted from the cooked fruit of the wild pomegranate (Naroli)	4	Chittaks
Black Sugar (*Gur*)	1	Seer
Hemp (*San*)	$1\frac{1}{4}$	"

201. It must be clearly understood that plaster such as that described above is only to be used on terraces, roofs, etc., where the original plaster of a more or less like kind has been preserved and is in need of repair. Ordinarily, terraces, roofs, etc., are to be repaired with concrete (paras. 97 and 229), over which no finishing coat is to be laid.

POINTING.

202. Lime mortar only, unless otherwise specified, is to be used for pointing, and it is essential that in repointing old buildings the instructions given below should be carefully followed in order that the best results may be obtained. In the case of new masonry, provided that it is laid in lime, it is better that the joints should be finished off at once.

203. The joints of the walls should be deeply raked out, to get rid of all loose dirt or old mortar, and to destroy the roots of weeds, grasses, or jungle which may be growing in them.

204. Old mortar, though apparently sound, often has a number of small voids behind the outer surface. When this is the case, these should be thoroughly exposed and the surface mortar cut out.

205. After cutting out (and before pointing) the joints should be very thoroughly blown out by an air-pump, or by using the pressure from the grouting machine, if it is on the building. They should then be washed out thoroughly with clean water, by means of a garden syringe or spraying machine, or by a hose-pipe when the latter is possible, or by using the grouting machine under pressure. The bricks or stones should be quite wet when the pointing is commenced. Care should be taken that no bulk of water remains lying in old hollows and fractures in the walls. POINTING—*contd.*

206. Where the raking out exceeds 3 inches in depth, the joints are, before pointing, to be tamped with cement mortar well pressed home with special tools (see Plate VII, fig. 3). The cement mortar is to be kept back a minimum of 2 inches from the face of the wall, or is to be raked out to that minimum depth. In either case it is to be left rough as a key for the lime pointing. Only so much of the masonry (about a super-yard) is to be tamped at one time as will permit of the pointing being done while the cement is still green.

207. Unless otherwise specified, the new mortar used for pointing should be made to harmonize with the old work adjacent both in colour and texture, fine gravel, *bajri*, pounded brick or other ingredients being used for the purpose, according to the instructions of the Archæological Officer. The mortar is to be rammed tightly home by means of wood or iron punches and modelling tools. Each joint should be finished off at once, and successive layers of the mortar should be avoided.

POINTING—*contd.* 208. Where grouting is required at the back of the pointing, the depth of the pointing should be at least 3 inches, and, where possible 5 to 6 inches in depth, including the tamped cement mortar.

209. The surface finish of the pointing will be decided by the Archæological Officer. In all cases it will be expected that the grit in the mortar shall show on the surface. This may be attained either by dashing clean water from a brush on to the pointing, or by pouring clean water from a tin on to it after it has begun to set, stubbing the pointing with a hog's hair brush and cleaning off with more water poured over it from the tin. Where it is imperative not to stain the masonry or brickwork on account of its colour, the surface of the pointing must be stubbed with a hog's hair brush, while a damp cloth is held along the lower edge of the joint. In cases like the latter very little water can be used.

210. During hot, or dry windy weather, the green pointing should be kept permanently damp for a period of two weeks, by covering the walls with damp cloths, and an awning, or by spraying with water from a spraying machine* as many times daily as may be necessary. In very wet weather the new mortar must be protected by tarpaulins or other efficient covering. The overseer is to see that the contractor arranges for the adequate protection or spraying of green pointing during holidays.

---

* The spraying machines recommended are those manufactured by the Four Oaks Spraying Machine Co., Sutton Coldfield, Birmingham, England.

211. Pointing must not in any circumstances be carried out during frosty weather, and, in cold districts, all work must be stopped one month before the period of the usual frosts of the district. Any work which is unavoidably carried out in seasons liable to frosts must be covered up at night with felt boards, sacking or other approved non-conducting materials. POINTING—*contd.*

212. In pointing the face of a wall the masons should start at the top and work downwards.

213. No pointing of any kind is to be keyed or struck with the trowel, but a perfectly flat face should be obtained for the joint between each stone and a rounded or lumpy surface must be avoided. It is not desired, however, that the surface should be so smooth that the grains of sand or *surkhi* are flush with the lime, but the grains should be made to stand out slightly beyond the lime face. A small sample of pointing will be supplied upon application to the Archæological Superintendent.

214. Where the masonry is uneven and the edge of one stone is recessed some distance back from an adjoining stone, the pointing, nevertheless, must still retain a flat face.

215. In ashlar work the pointing material should be well pressed back with a flat tool, so that the mortar face may be approximately at right angles to the beds of the masonry, in order to avoid a feather edge in the mortar. In every case instructions should be given by the Archæological Superintendent as to whether the pointing is to be flush or recessed, and if the latter to what extent.

POINTING—*concld.* 216. In pointing up very wide joints in masonry, pieces of stone which roughly fill up the open space may be inserted, as shown in Fig. 4, Plate VII. These stones should have a weathered face to match the old work. Filling up the wide joints with small stones, as shown in Fig. 5, Plate VII, will not be permitted.

217. All stones inserted in this manner are to have, at least, a 4-inch bed.

218. When a new brick or stone wall is being built in lime mortar, or where a new face in lime mortar is being added to a decayed wall, the pointing is to be finished as the work proceeds, and the joints must not first be raked out and then pointed. Where the wall or new face is built in cement the instructions in para. 206 are to be followed.

219. In India, "pointing" is frequently understood to mean the smearing of mortar flush over the surfaces on either side of a joint, and the subsequent marking of the line of the joint by an incised line. Such "pointing" must never be permitted on an ancient monument. It is an anachronism which cannot be too strongly guarded against.

220. In monuments of the pre-Muhammadan period, mortar was almost unknown. If in their reconstruction or repair its use is unavoidable, it should never be visible on the surface of the masonry or brickwork.

REBUILDING. 221. When the core of a wall is found to be either full of earth or disintegrated or dry built, it may be necessary to remove some of the face stones in order to clean out the dirt. This should only be done under special instructions from the Archæological Officer, and before putting the work in hand each stone should be numbered, and a diagram or photo prepared, showing the numbering (see para. 189), in order that the stones may be replaced in their original positions. After the removal of the face stones the core of the wall should be thoroughly raked or washed out and loose mortar or dirt extracted. The backs and joints of the stones should then be cleaned and they should be replaced in their correct positions, rebedded in cement or lime mortar, and pointed up as previously described with lime mortar. REBUILDING—*contd.*

222. No wall is to be taken down without the express permission of the Archæological Superintendent.

223. Where face stones are so badly perished and fractured that the core of the wall is in danger of being exposed, fresh stone may have to be inserted.

224. Modern stones with modern tooling should not be inserted in old work except under instructions from the Archæological Superintendent.

225. Where a new face has to be added to a decayed stone wall, it must be properly and efficiently secured to the main structure with bond stones. The length of the end projecting into the old work will vary according to circumstances, but should be at least 12 inches. The bond stones should be spaced, as a rule, 3 feet apart horizontally and 12 inches vertically.

226. Where the face of the masonry is very uneven and some stones have been worn away for a considerable distance back from those adjoining, the recessed stones may be loosened and be brought out to align with the true face of the masonry; the cavity behind should then be filled up. This work must not, however, be

carried out without the express instructions of the Archæological Superintendent.

Roofs and Domes.

227. All accumulations of soil or débris on terraced roofs or other flat surfaces are to be removed, since they favour the growth of vegetation. Any opening in roofs through which rainwater can percolate are to be stopped or covered in, and proper drainage provided.

228. Cracks and fractures in ancient plaster covering terraced or sloping roofs or domes are to be treated as specified in para. 102 (see also para. 199). In all cases in which the new work is visible, it is to be coloured to match the surfaces adjoining, the colouring materials being mixed with the plaster and not applied after the repairs are done.

229. If the old plaster is so disintegrated that a complete recovering of the roof is unavoidable, a concrete should be used for the purpose which may be either (*a*) cement concrete as specified in para. 97, or (*b*) lime concrete to which cement in the proportion of 1 : 9 of lime has been added. In either case the nature and size of the aggregate and the thickness of the coat are to be determined by the Engineer in charge, and in either case colouring matter is to be added as specified for plaster in paras. 199 and 200.

230. Where concrete is used for the covering of roofs and domes, it is to be finished in accordance with the instructions given for terraced flooring in M. W. H., p. 36. On no account is a finishing coat of plaster to be laid over the concrete.

231. If a roof or dome requiring repair is covered with brick or stone, the outer course of bricks or stones

should be removed and reset in cement mortar, waterproofed, if necessary, as specified in para. 193.

232. If it is neccssary to construct modern roofs for the protection of sculptures or other antiquities left *in situ*, full particulars as to the type of roof required and its construction should be given by the Archæological Superintendent, who should consider each case on its own merits and with special reference to the materials locally available and to the propriety of the proposed roof amid the surroundings in which it is to be placed. MODERN ROOFS ON ANCIENT SITES.

233. Sand used in the making of mortar should be *coarse*-grained, perfectly clean, sharp, and preferably of a yellow and variegated colour. It should, if possible, be obtained from local pits, rivers or seashores, but it is absolutely essential that it should possess the above-mentioned qualities, in order that a successful result may be obtained for cement or lime mortar. Fine-grained, dusty, or dirty sand must not be allowed, and each fresh consignment should be carefully inspected in order to see that it corresponds with the sample approved in the first case. SAND.

234. Many sands, which would otherwise be of good quality, contain lumps of foreign matter, or a quantity of dusty particles. Such sand may, with the Engineer's consent, be used after it has been thoroughly sifted and washed.

235. Sea-sand contains a quantity of salt which will cause efflorescence when the mortar is set. The salt must be eliminated by very thorough washing in clean water, the water being renewed at each washing.

The amount of salt in the sand can be judged roughly by tasting the water in which it has been washed.

STONEWORK, NEW—

236. New stonework which has to be inserted in ancient structures, should be matched as nearly as possible with the old masonry adjoining it. It frequently happens that the same quarry yields several varieties of stone, and care should, therefore, be taken when putting in new patches to procure stone of the same texture and colour as was used by the original builders.

STAINING OF STONEWORK.

237. In some cases, where the old stonework has weathered to a darker tint, it may be desirable, in order to avoid any violent and unpleasant contrast between the new and old surfaces, to resort to artificial means of staining the former. Such staining, however, should not be attempted in any situation where it will be exposed to heavy and prolonged rains, since no stain has yet been discovered which will successfully withstand them, even for one season.

238. In sheltered positions and in dry climates, the following stains have been found efficacious.

(*a*) Bark of acacia . . . . ½ seer.
Cement . . . . ½ chittak.

Boil the bark of acacia in 5 seers of water until reduced to half the quantity, then mix with it cement and as much powdered murum (generally about 2 chittaks) and as much powdered charcoal and, if necessary, cowdung as may be needed to obtain the requisite colour. Apply the stain with a brush.

(*b*) *Bhilawan nut* (pounded) . . . . ½ seer.
Methylated spirit . . . . . 2 seers.

Mix pounded *bhilawan* nut with the methylated spirit and keep the mixture for two days before it is used. Apply with a brush.

239. In all cases the staining of stonework must be carried out under the personal supervision of an Archæological Officer.

STONE PRESERVATIVES.

240. No experiments are to be tried with any stone preservative on ancient buildings except under instructions from the Archæological Superintendent. The latter should in all cases consult the Archæological Chemist before recommending any particular preservative, and should supply him, if possible, with a specimen of the weathered stone, so that he may test chemically for the causes of decomposition. No known preservative is suitable for all stones or for all kinds of decay; and no patent solutions on the market are as efficacious as they are claimed to be. If in any case the Archæological Chemist advises the use of Baryta water or other solutions injurious to man, the overseer must see that the workmen adopt the precautions recommended in order to avoid the evil effects to which they would otherwise be exposed.

ROCK SULPHUR.

241. Rock sulphur is melted down in a manner similar to lead, a small kettle being a convenient utensil. When boiling it is poured round and into the joint, using clay in the same way as when lead is employed.

242. Sulphur is very inflammable, and care has to be taken when heating, as once on fire great difficulty is experienced in extinguishing it. It does not flame, but only smoulders.

TILEWORK.

243. Where pieces of tilework have fallen away, leaving gaps in the surface, the gaps should not be

TILEWORK—*contd.* filled with plaster, but the tiles adjoining the gaps should be edged round with a neat fillet of plaster as specified in para. 198. The plaster should be coloured so as to harmonize with the exposed ground on which the tiles are bedded, not to match the tiles, themselves.

UNDERPINNING. 244. All excavations for underpinning must be carefully and adequately planked and strutted, and all the masonry work, etc., immediately above the proposed stretch of underpinning, must be adequately held by raking shores on a good solid foundation.

245. Where a long length of wall has to be underpinned, the work must be carried out in sections about 3 feet in width, and to the depth indicated in the estimate; the masonry overhead and the earth at the sides must be thoroughly shored up and strutted.

246. If the underpinning exceeds three feet in height, the masonry is to be built up in layers not exceeding two feet, and each layer is to be allowed to set before the layer above it is added.

247. Two sections may be carried out together, but under no circumstances should they adjoin; generally a distance of 12 feet should separate any two such sections. The holes must be kept quite free from water by pumping or bailing out.

248. If the underpinning is to be in concrete (see para. 97) from the foundation level up to the underside of the wall, temporary rough-boarded centering must be placed across the outer face of the hole, the boards being placed in position as the concrete is filled in. If the ground is of a loose or sandy nature, close boarded sheeting must be placed on all sides round the

hole. All such boarding should be covered with a coat of limewash on the sides adjacent to the concrete to prevent the latter adhering. UNDERPINNING—*contd.*

249. All concrete must be well rammed into a dense solid mass when possible, and where the height of the hole is insufficient to ram vertically, the concrete must be well punned in from the front face. Where there is any difficulty in punning up to the underside of the foundations, the interstices must be filled up with cement grout, if possible, from the grouting machine.

250. Where the footings of the walls are very loose and disintegrated, the joints should be well washed out and filled with cement grout, if possible, before the underpinning is commenced.

251. Where a section of the underpinning adjoins a previous section, the sides of the block of concrete are to be thoroughly washed and covered with a coat of cement grout applied with a brush.

252. Where the concrete underpinning will not be subjected to a heavy load (*e.g.*, in a thick low wall) the cost may be reduced by the insertion of fairly large pieces of stone in the body of the concrete. All such stones should be bedded flat and must be washed clean before being laid.

253. In removing weeds, trees or shrubs, etc., from walls it is essential that the roots should be completely destroyed, and during the process of raking out any tendrils found in the joints should be followed up and removed. The growth of vegetation in the joints of ancient brick or stone buildings is one of the principal factors in causing their ruin, and the only sure way VEGETATION (JUNGLE).

VEGETATION (JUNGLE)—*contd.*

of dealing with this evil is constantly to eradicate the plants before they become fully rooted.

254. Joints which have to be raked out in order to destroy the vegetation should, after the earth, etc., has been removed, be immediately repointed (see paras. 202 *sqq.*).

255. The cutting out of large trees from ancient masonry is an operation that demands especial care. As a rule, large trees should be removed in sections, in order to prevent injury being done to the masonry.

256. When jungle has to be cleared from around an ancient monument, it should be cut for at least 30 yards on all sides, unless special reasons to the contrary exist, and its roots should be completely eradicated so as to prevent them from sprouting again.

WALL ENDS.

257. Where wall ends are composed of small stones, not large enough on bed to permit the joints to be raked, the stones, may, on instructions from the Archæological Superintendent, be removed and rebedded in cement or lime mortar.

WALL TOPS.

258. Tops of walls are to be treated only in accordance with instructions from the Archæological Superintendent, unless immediate measures are necessary for their security, in which case the steps taken are to be of a temporary character, and are in nowise to affect or alter the work existing.

259. Unless otherwise specified, pointing (and bedding where necessary) to wall tops is to be done in cement mortar made with coarse-grained sand, to which Medusa or Pudlo or other waterproofing materials may be added if considered necessary. The surface finishing is to be of the same character as in lime mortar.

260. Where the wall tops have a broken sky-line, this must be left, and on no account be straightened, unless there are special reasons for restoration. Such restoration must only be carried out under written instructions from the Archæological Superintendent. WALL TOPS—*contd.*

261. Where the tops consist of large firm stones well weathered, and the joints are clean, it will probably only be necessary to point. Where, however, as in the majority of cases, the tops consist of loose stones with dirty joints, or where hollows holding rain water occur, the work is to be undertaken in small sections. The stones are to be numbered, and a rough diagram is to be made showing their position. The stones may then be lifted, and cleaned, and a layer of the cement mortar laid over the whole section to be treated. The stones are then to be rebedded in their exact position, care being taken to preserve all the irregularities that existed before the top was touched, provided always that no hollows are left for the retention of water.

262. Low foundation or other walls, especially those exposed in excavations, may sometimes be protected by a covering of earth or grass. In such cases the Archæological Superintendent must satisfy himself that the protection given will be adequate and that means can be taken to prevent jungle growing in the earth.

263. If walls are out of plumb, it is seldom necessary to dismantle and rebuild them. In many cases it will be found that the fault was caused soon after the erection of the building by the subsidence of the foundations, which, having permanently settled, are not likely to go any further. If there is any suspicion WALLS OUT OF PLUMB.

WALLS OUT OF PLUMB—*contd.* of movement, the wall should be carefully watched and any movement reported.

WEATHER STAINS AND LICHENS. 264. Weather stains and lichens on the outside of a building should not ordinarily be removed, but any growths which are obscuring carvings or inscriptions or are open to objection on other grounds, may be removed by brushing with soap and water or by means of blunt wooden instruments. But care must be taken not to scratch the surface or to leave other unsightly marks of the cleaning, thus making the remedy worse than the defect.

265. Weather stains on white marble or stucco may be removed by the use of soda ash (caustic soda). The soda ash should be well mixed with chalk or lime and country soap, in a proportion of 10 to 25 per cent. of the other ingredients, and the mixture should be worked to the consistency of a thick paste which should then be lightly rubbed over the stains. About seven hours afterwards it should be washed off with warm water, the washings being repeated until the water fails to turn red litmus paper blue.

An alternative method is to dissolve 1 lb. of caustic soda in 1 gallon of water and apply in the case of marble with a soft bristle brush, in the case of stucco with a clean soft cloth, then after a few minutes to wash the surface thoroughly with clean water. The litmus paper test should invariably be applied to the washings to ensure that no trace of alkali remains on the cleaned surface.

WIRE NETTING. 266. In view of the costliness of expanded metal as compared with ordinary wire netting, the latter may be used wherever special strength is not required and where there are no objections to it on other grounds, *e.g.*, in window-opening high up in a building. WIRE NETTING—*contd.*

267. For doors in conspicuous positions an excellent kind of wire netting of various patterns and gauges can be obtained from Ahmedabad in the Bombay Presidency. Cf. Plate XV.

268. The principles applying to the conservation of wooden buildings must, owing to the nature of their material and the comparatively short duration of their existence, necessarily differ from the principles applying to structures in brick or stone. WOODWORK.

269. Once a brick or stone structure is put into a good state of repair, it may be expected that, with a little attention from time to time, it will last for several hundred years. With wooden structures this is far from being the case and, as a rule, the strictest economy must be observed in their conservation. In the treatment of many relatively modern buildings this may ordinarily be confined to (1) such plain structural repairs as will ensure the stability of the building, (2) repairs to the roof with a view to prevent the percolation of rain water, (3) oiling of the woodwork, and (4) such protective measures as are necessary to preserve the glass incrustate work or other ornaments.

270. On the other hand, no pains or expense should be spared in the preservation of any woodwork belonging to the mediæval or earlier ages, as specimens of this class of work are exceedingly rare and valuable, and one and all of them, whether they be complete structures, like the temples of the Chamba valley, or

WOODWORK—*concld.*

doors, pillars and the like, built into some stone or brick edifice, ought to be highly prized and scrupulously cared for. The treatment of such woodwork, if it is to be successful, may be a difficult and technical matter, and the assistance of the Archæological Chemist should, as a rule, be invoked.

271. For the preservation of teak wood, periodic applications of crude earth oil or boiled linseed oil are efficacious. For other kinds of wood "Solignum" is generally preferable.

272. Woodwork found in wet soil or water should not be exposed to the air, but should be kept in water or wet sand or wet sawdust pending receipt of instructions as to its treatment from the Archæological Chemist. Before being laid in wet sand or sawdust, painted, carved or inscribed parts should be protected by a layer of cotton wool. These precautions are necessary to prevent shrinkage and distortion of the wood through too rapid drying.

273. If woodwork is found to be infected with injurious insects, the pest may be destroyed by means of carbon disulphide or hydrocyanic acid, the wood being afterwards protected against further damage by the application of a suitable preservative.

INDEX.

For insertion in the Conservation Manual by Sir John Marshall.

General Rules for the treatment of Stone Buildings with Preservative solutions.

In order to employ a stone preservative to the best advantage, it is important to observe the following rules carefully :—

(*a*) The surface which requires the treatment should be quite clean. Any foreign deposits, such as dust, soot, etc., should be removed by a brush, which should not be so hard as to injure the stone. If necessary, soap and hot water may be used, but coatings of oil, colour or former preservatives will have to be eliminated by special treatments. The operation should aim at freeing the pores of all obstructions before the application of the stone preservative.

(*b*) The surface should be quite dry. This rule applies also if the treatment has to be repeated, (*vide* c).

(*c*) The application of the stone preservative should be repeated three or more times until no more is absorbed. The first coating requires a very dilute solution which will penetrate as deep as possible, and, on drying, leave the pores still free to receive more of the preservative. The concentration of the subsequent coatings may be gradually increased.

(*d*) The preservative should penetrate the surface as deep as possible. In order to facilitate this, the solution, and if possible, the surface also, should be warmed before the application.

(*e*) The surface should be cleaned with a moist sponge, immediately after each treatment in order to remove any superfluous preservative and keep the surface clean. If this precaution is neglected the surface, on drying, will appear unsightly and more or less glossy.

(*f*) Round stiff paint brushes are suitable for applications on plain surfaces but a sprayer will be more handy for reliefs or ornamentations.

(*g*) The nozzle of the sprayer should be held as near the surface as practicable and the solutions (employed with the sprayer) should be more dilute than those for application with brushes. The reason being, that the rate of evaporation from fine drops is much greater than that from a plane surface, and it is desirable that the solution should not get concentrated on reaching the stone surface.

(*h*) The quantity of a preservative which is prepared at a time should not be more than what can be consumed in a short time. This is due to the fact that some preservatives are affected by the atmosphere and the solution will become concentrated by the loss of its volatile constituents. At the end of the operation the brushes, sprayer and utensils should be cleaned and left to dry.

(i) The weather should be warm and dry. The amount of moisture retained by a stone surface depends on the humidity and temperature of the atmosphere. If the treatment is carried out in moist weather, the preservative solution will not penetrate sufficiently and, on drying, form a thin hard layer near the surface, which will peel off in course of time. Moreover, in hot weather the enclosed moisture will tend to escape through this hard layer and help in its disintegration. The surface should not be exposed to the direct rays of the sun at the time of treatment.

These are the more important and general precautions, which should be supplemented by the directions which the proprietors specially recommend for their preparations. There will still be sufficient room for the sound judgment and skilful manipulation of the operator. In any case it is very desirable to carry out preliminary experiments on unimportant parts of the monument.

SGPI—S17—X-3(14)—2-11-23—2,000..

PLATE I.

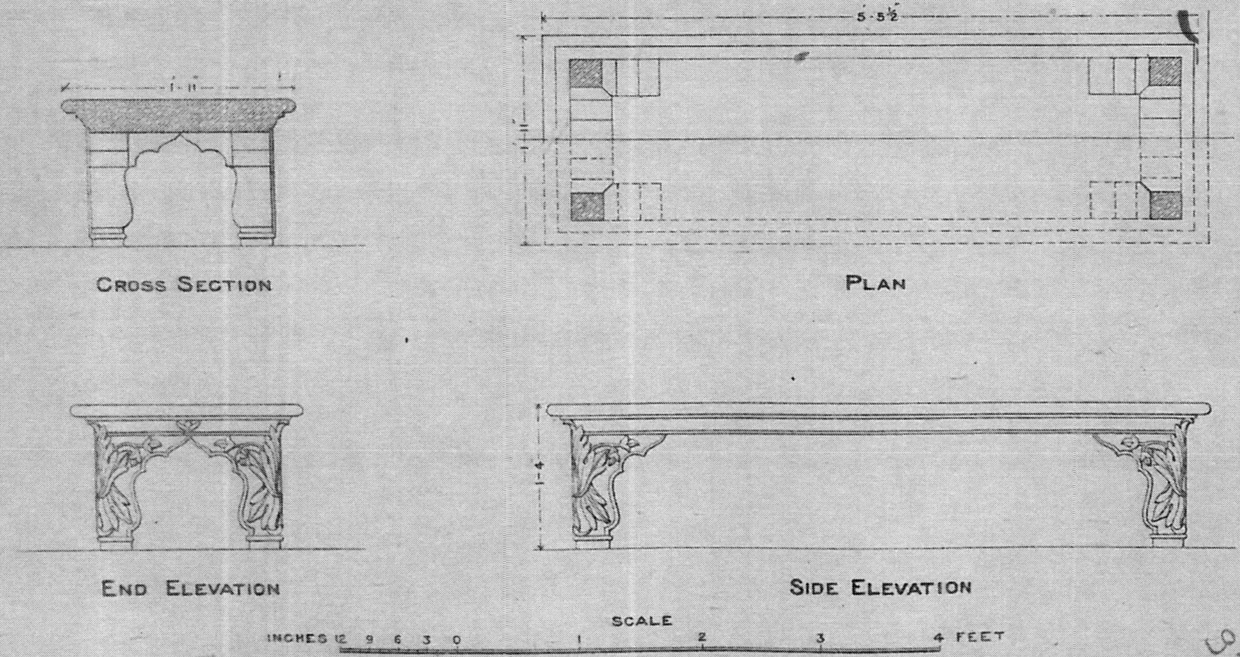

MUGHAL SEATS OF MARBLE AND SANDSTONE AT TAJ MAHAL, AGRA. (See para. 81).

HELIO S. I. O. CALCUTTA.

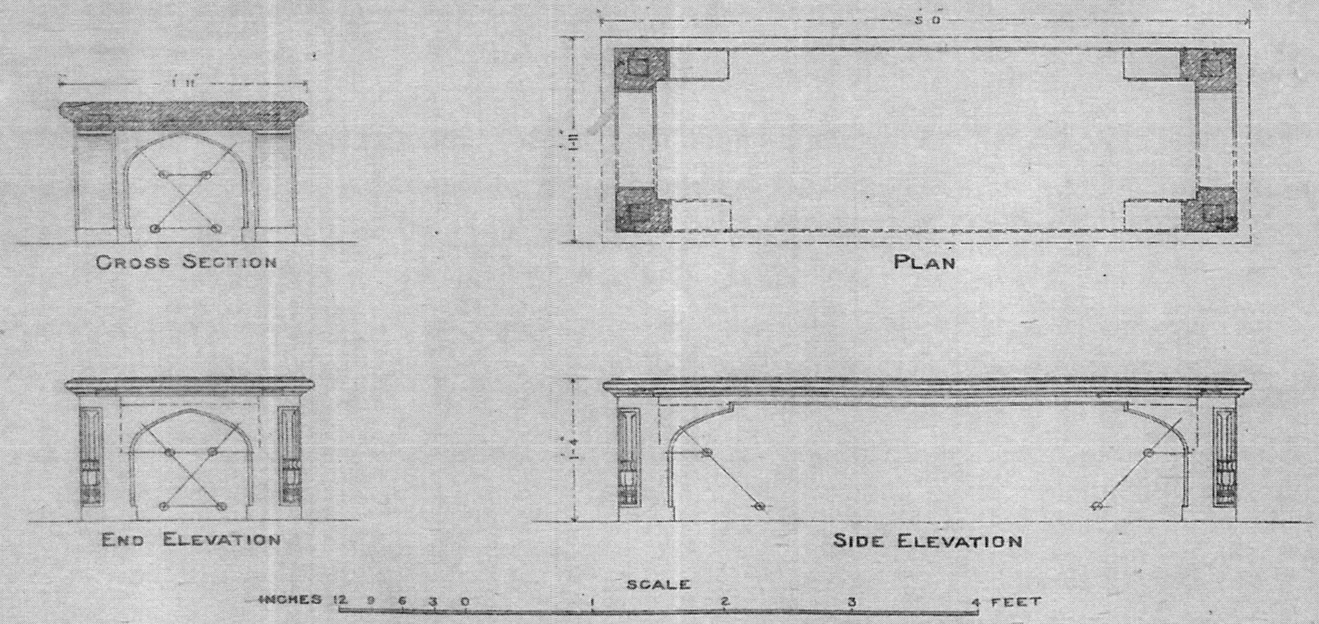

SANDSTONE SEATS OF EARLY MUGHAL PATTERN AT HUMAYUN'S TOMB, DELHI. (See para. 81).

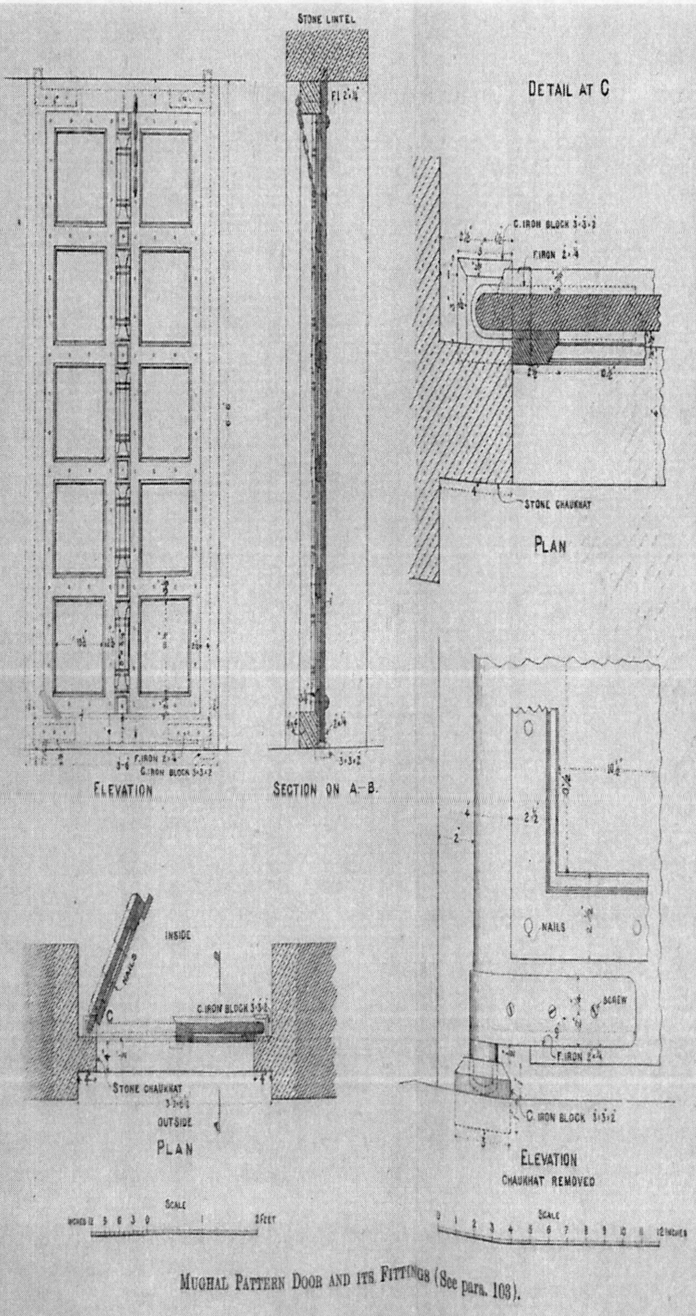

MUGHAL PATTERN DOOR AND ITS FITTINGS (See para. 103).

Plate IV.

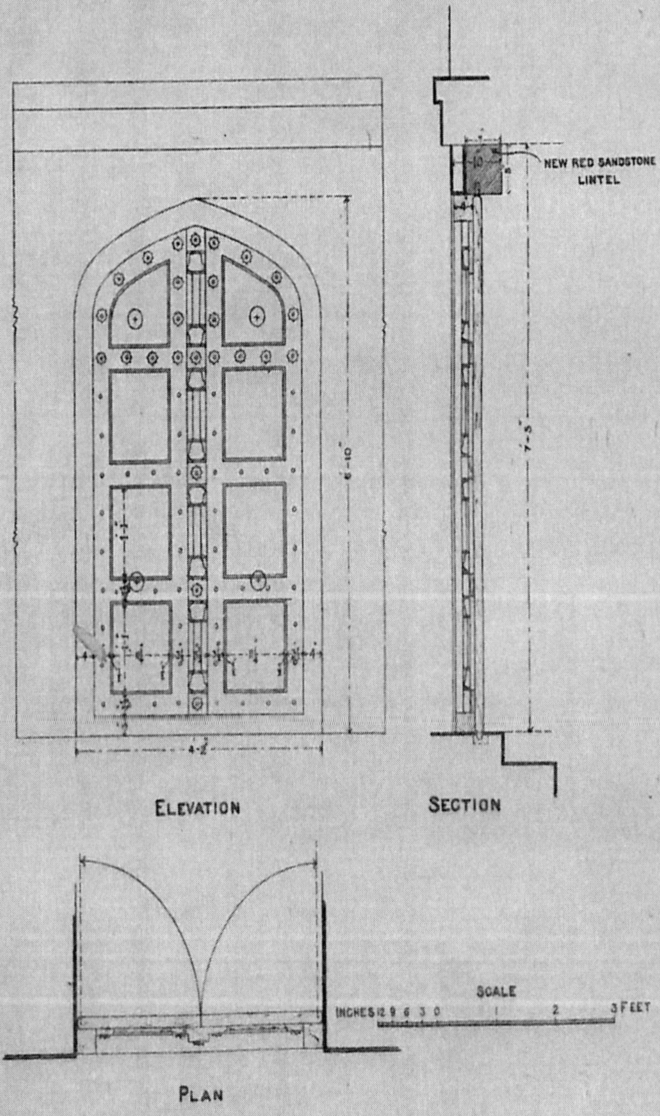

Mughal Door in Delhi Fort (See para. 103).

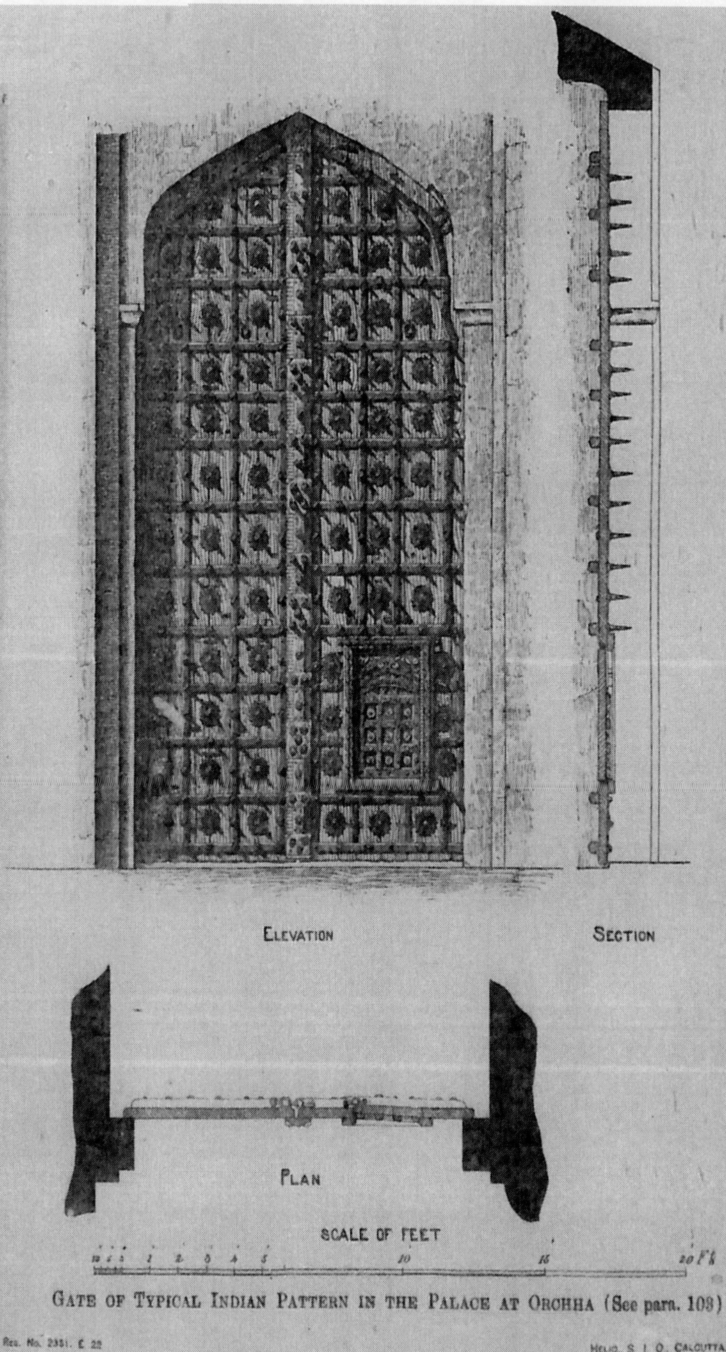

GATE OF TYPICAL INDIAN PATTERN IN THE PALACE AT ORCHHA (See para. 108)

Reg. No. 2351. E 22

Helio. S. I. O. Calcutta

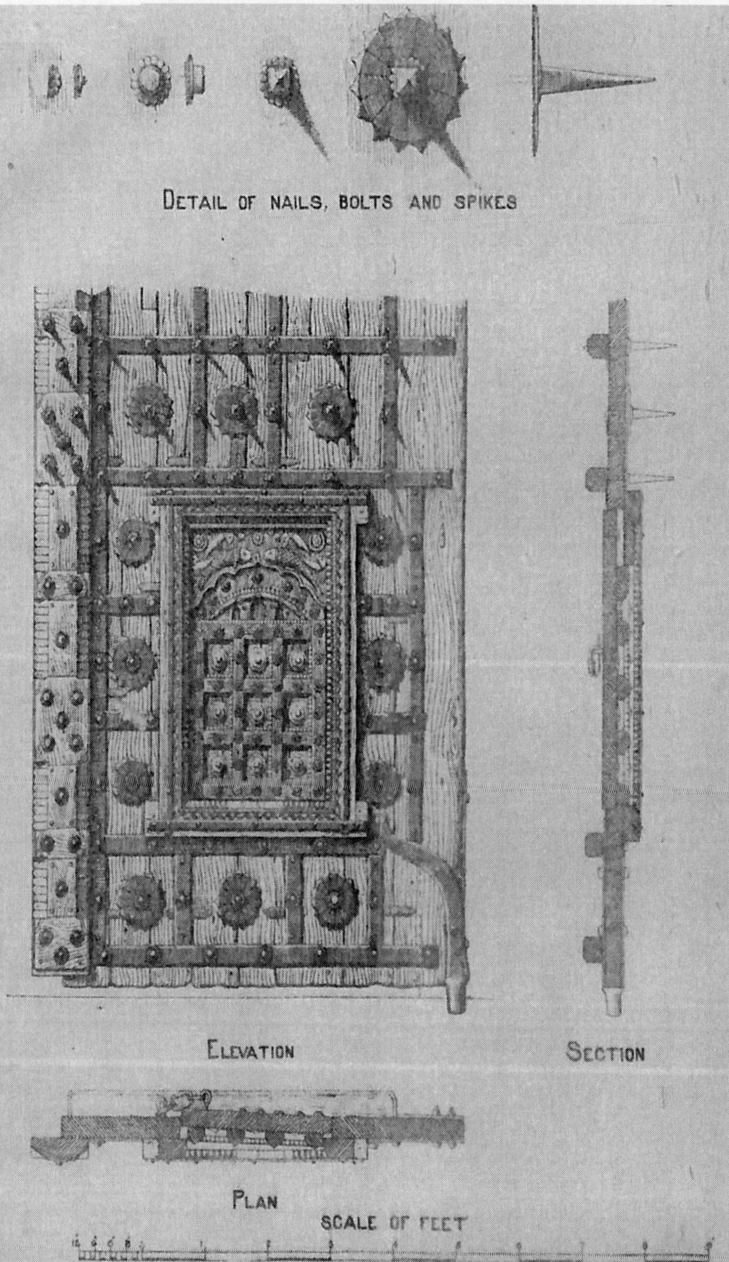

DETAIL OF GATE IN THE PALACE AT ORCHHA (See para. 103).

PLATE VII.

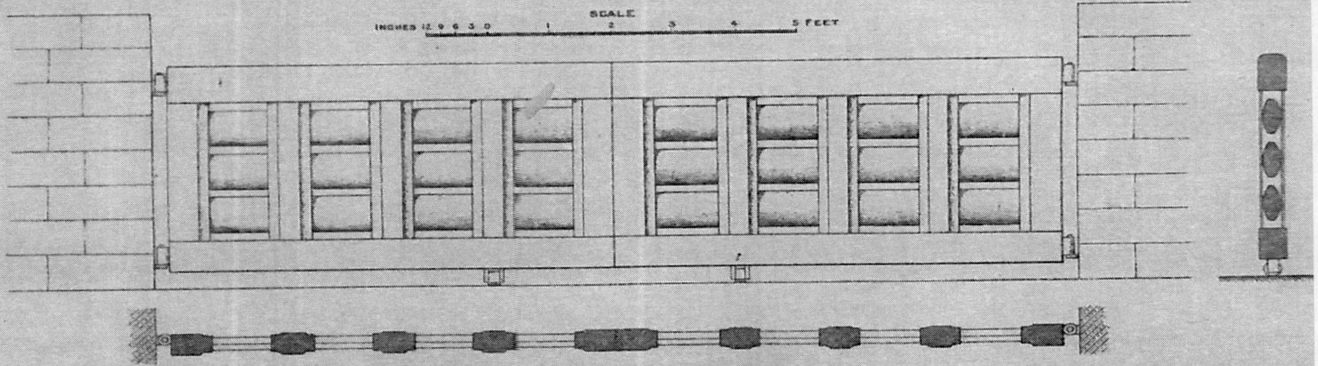

TEAK WOOD GATE OF BUDDHIST "RAIL" PATTERN AT SANCHI (See para. 103).

FIG. 1

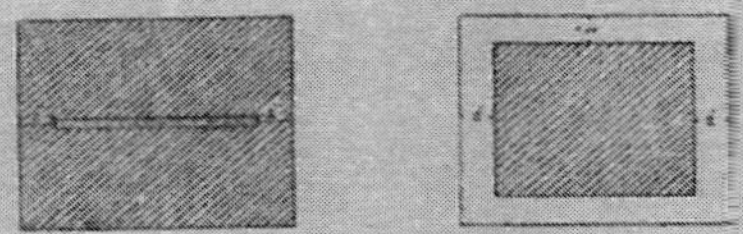

SECTION. PLAN.

FIG. 2

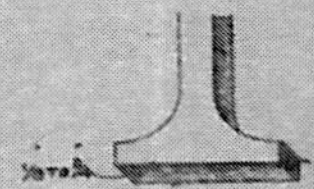

FLAT TAMPING TOOL.

FIG. 3

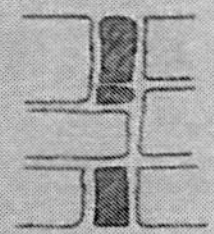

FIG. 4

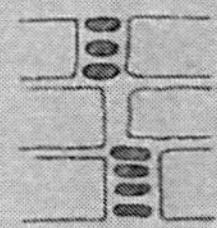

FIG 5

HELIO S I O CALCUTTA

PLATE VIII.

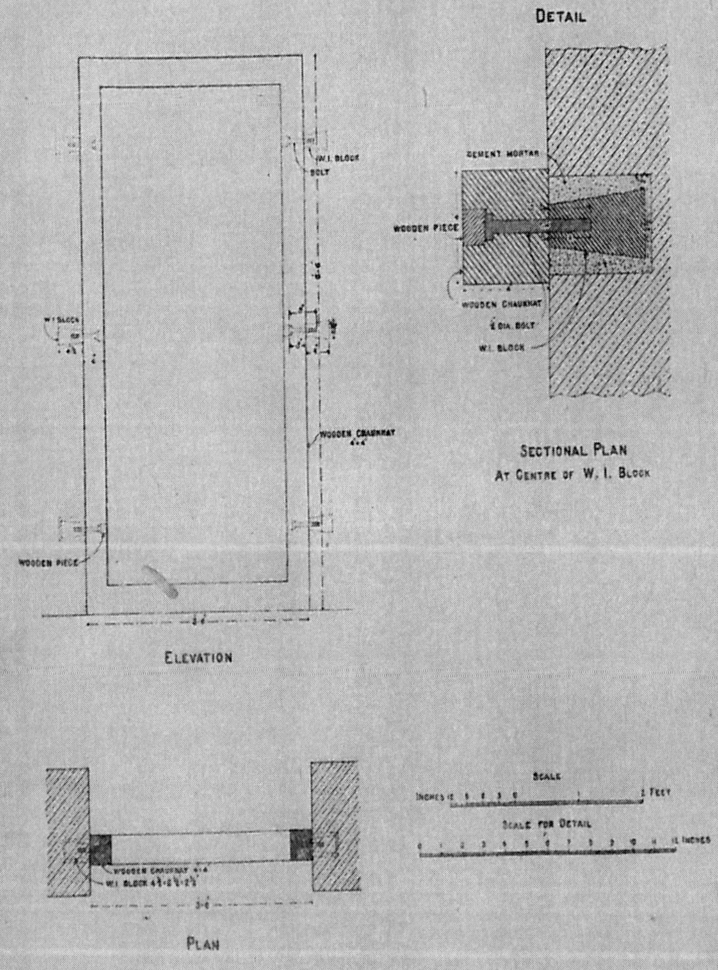

METHOD OF FIXING DOOR-FRAME IN OPENINGS OF STONE (See para. 103).

Reg. No. 2361. E. 22 HELIO. S. I. O. CALCUTTA

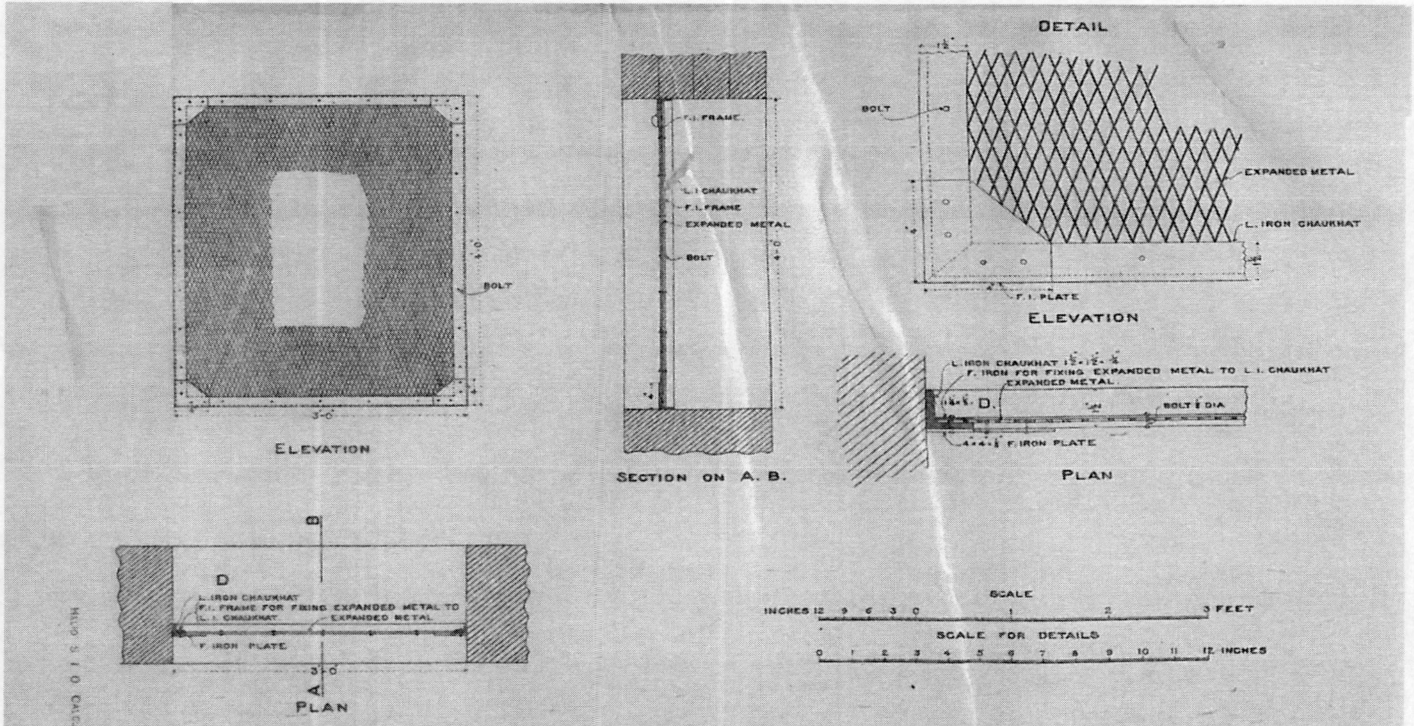

METHOD OF FIXING EXPANDED METAL TO ANGLE-IRON FRAME (See para. 104).

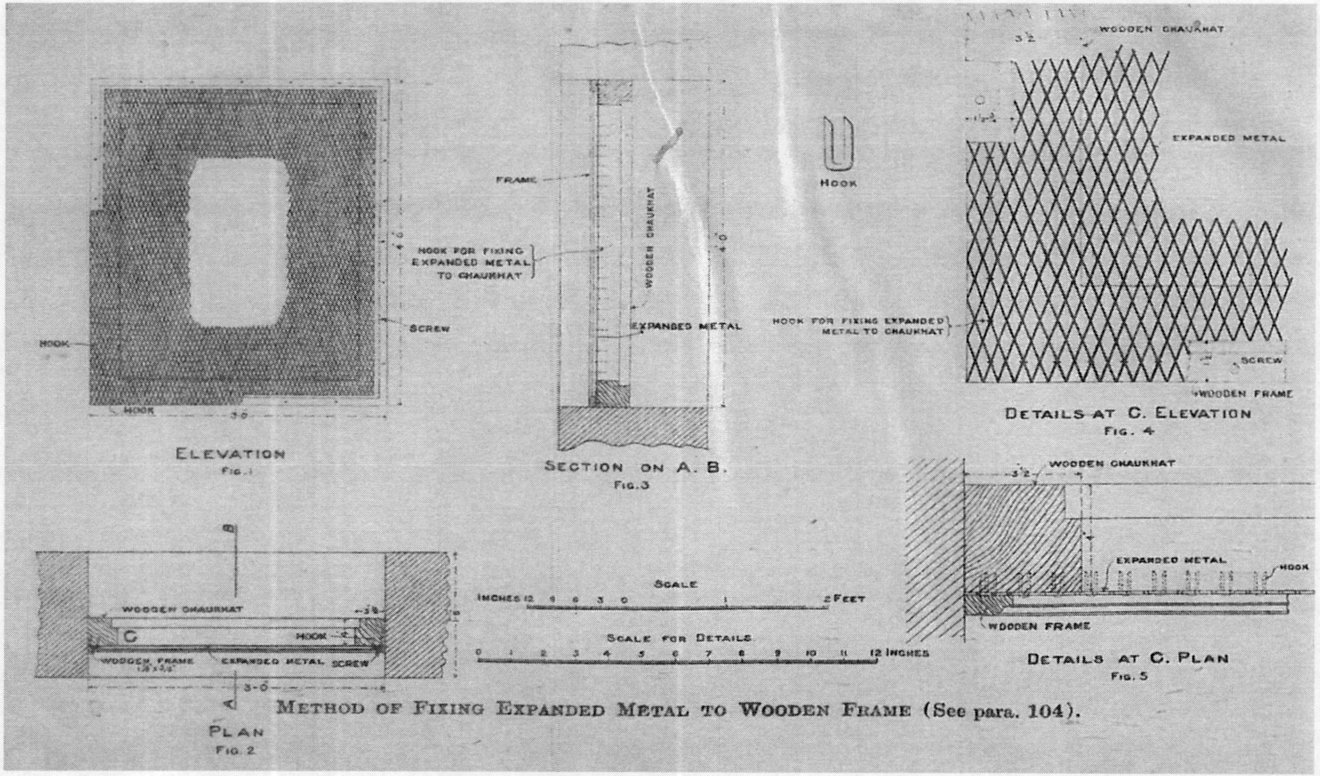

METHOD OF FIXING EXPANDED METAL TO WOODEN FRAME (See para. 104).

PLATE XI.

GROUTING MACHINE AT WORK (SEE PARA. 147).

Photo.-engraved & printed at the Offices of the Survey of India, Calcutta, 1922.

PLATE XII.

N.B.—THE SIZE OF THE STIRRUP AND ROLLED STEEL JOIST TO BE CALCULATED IN EACH CASE.

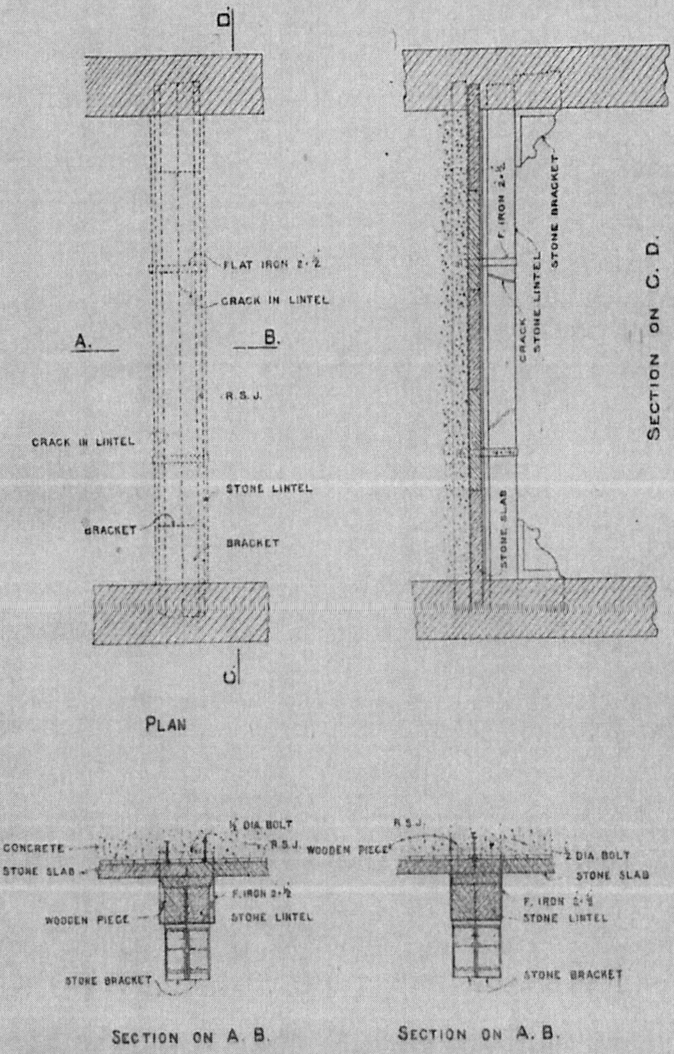

METHOD OF STIRRUPING OLD BROKEN BEAMS (See para. 186).

Reg. No. 2351 E 22

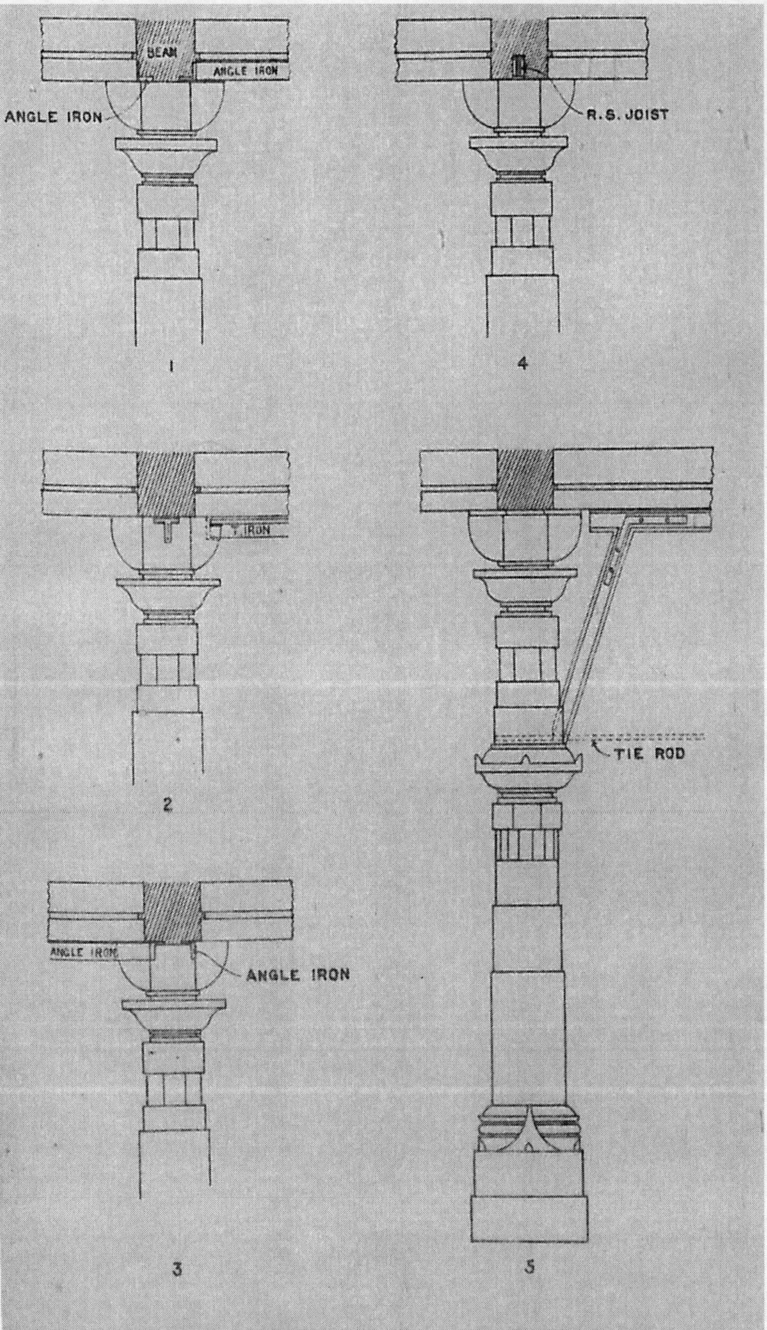

OTHER DEVICES FOR SUPPORTING BROKEN BEAMS (See para. 186).

Plate XIV.

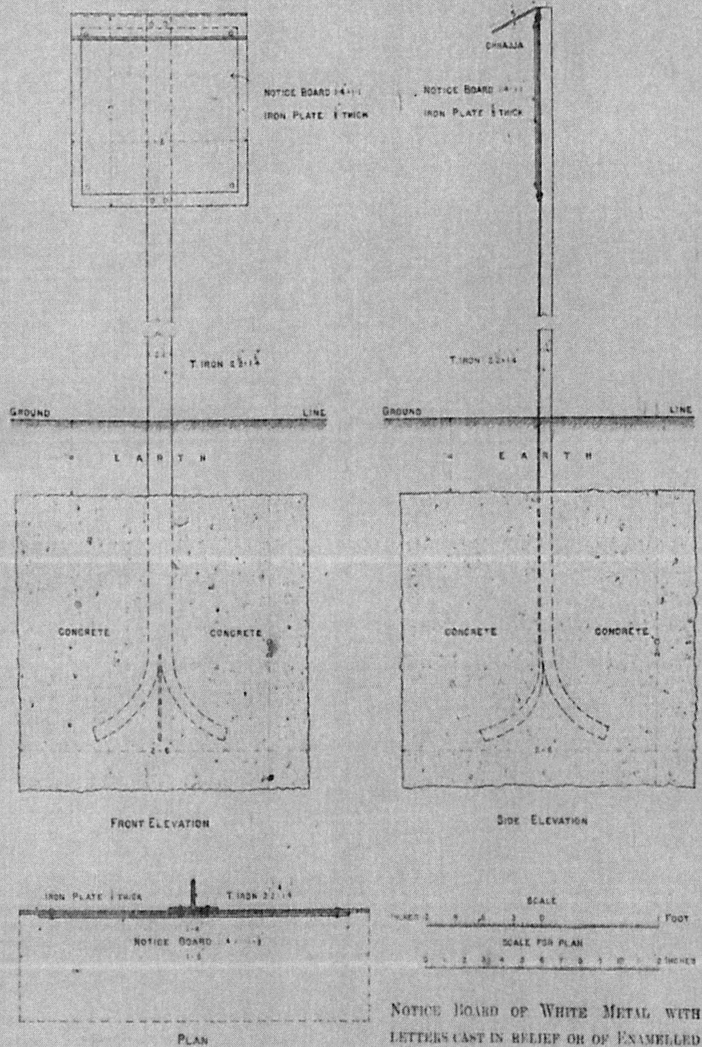

Notice Board of White Metal with letters cast in relief or of Enamelled Iron. Standard of T-iron Imbedded in Concrete Foundation (See para. 190).

Reg. No. 2251. E 22

M. I. G. S. I. O. Calcutta

SPECIMEN OF AHMADABAD WIRE NETTING (See para. 267).

Reg. No. 2351, E. 22—2,000

Photo. S. I. O. Calcutta